*The Samuel & Alt*hea Stroum Lectures

IN JEWISH

The Samuel & Althea Stroum Lectures

IN JEWISH STUDIES

Popular Culture and the Shaping of Holocaust Memory in America

ALAN MINTZ

UNIVERSITY OF WASHINGTON PRESS

Seattle and London

Library of Congress Cataloging-in-Publication Data

Mintz, Alan L.
    Popular culture and the shaping of Holocaust memory in America/
Alan Mintz.
        p.   cm.—(Samuel and Althea Stroum lectures in Jewish studies)
    Includes index.
    ISBN 0-295-98120-2 (alk. paper)
    1. Holocaust, Jewish (1939–1945)—Foreign public opinion, American.
2. Holocaust, Jewish (1939–1945)—Influence.   3. Holocaust, Jewish
(1939–1945)—Historiography.   4. Holocaust, Jewish (1939–1945),
in motion pictures.   5. Judgment at Nuremberg (Motion picture)
6. Pawnbroker (Motion picture)   7. Schindler's list (Motion picture)
8. Jews—United States—Attitudes.   9. Public opinion—United States.
I. Title.   II. Series.

D804.45.U55 P67   2001
940.53'18—dc21   2001027016

The Samuel & Althea Stroum Lectures

IN JEWISH STUDIES

Samuel Stroum, businessman, community leader, and philanthropist, by a major gift to the Jewish Federation of Greater Seattle,
established the Samuel and Althea Stroum Philanthropic Fund.

In recognition of Mr. and Mrs. Stroum's deep interest in Jewish
history and culture, the Board of Directors of the Jewish Federation
of Greater Seattle, in cooperation with the Jewish Studies Program
of the Henry M. Jackson School of International Studies at the
University of Washington, established an annual lectureship at the
University of Washington known as the Samuel and Althea Stroum
Lectureship in Jewish Studies. This lectureship makes it possible
to bring to the area outstanding scholars and interpreters of Jewish
thought, thus promoting a deeper understanding of Jewish history, religion, and culture. Such understanding can lead to an
enhanced appreciation of the Jewish contributions to the historical
and cultural traditions that have shaped the American nation.

The terms of the gift also provide for the publication from
time to time of the lectures or other appropriate materials resulting from or related to the lectures.

For Baruch Goldstein
Tsaddik Bedorotav

Contents

Preface

My path to the subject of this study was indirect, and this very indirection is in large measure what the book is about. I am a student of Hebrew literature, and some years ago, in an effort to understand the dialectic between tradition and modernity, I traced the literary responses to catastrophic events in Jewish history, beginning with the destruction of the Jerusalem temples and ending with the destruction of European Jewry in our time. When it came to the response in Israeli literature to the Holocaust, it became clear that the complexity of this phenomenon could be grasped only in the context of the Zionist revolution that had given birth to Israel and its ideological repudiations of traditional paradigms. Viewing this literature as being essentially an Israeli branch of an international literature of the Holocaust, while yielding some insights, seemed to be very wide of the mark. Israeli culture had admitted the Holocaust very much on its own terms, and unless the embroiled nature of those terms—which involved all sorts of denial and displacement—was adequately understood, the hope of grasping the true significance of these works was remote.

As interest in the Holocaust heightened in the subsequent years, I found myself increasingly uneasy with the way in which works of Holocaust culture were talked about as if they formed a world unto

Preface

themselves, possessing their own laws and poetics. In the course I developed on Holocaust literature at Brandeis University I tried to correct this imbalance by stressing the national and linguistic context of the works we read and the distinct cultural lenses through which different victims of the Holocaust had perceived and framed their experience. When I was invited by the University of Washington to deliver the Samuel and Althea Stroum Lectures, I was afforded an opportunity to turn my attention to the reception of the Holocaust in America and to test the applicability of what I had learned in my study of Israeli culture. I thus turn my attention to the Americanization of the Holocaust as a specialist in neither Holocaust studies nor American studies but rather as a visitor from another field who hopes to make a contribution because he comes from the outside. I speak also as a cultural critic and an American Jew who, like many others, is concerned for the future of Holocaust remembrance in America.

Each of the four chapters in this volume aims to accomplish a different purpose and is written in a different mode. Chapter 1, "From Silence to Salience," which is written in a synoptic style with few references to primary and secondary sources, offers a general account of the journey of the Holocaust from the margins to the center of public discourse in America. The Holocaust is an event that took place far from the United States and involved few Americans; yet this is an event that, unlike all others, has loomed larger with the passage of time rather than waning. This is a complex phenomenon that requires explanation from many angles. Chapter 1 presents a synthetic interpretation of the phenomenon as a whole that stresses the particular angle of vision followed in this study: the pivotal role of popular culture in spreading awareness of the Holocaust from the Jewish community to the larger American nation. I stress the status of this chapter as an interpretation because I recognize that there are many legitimate approaches to a question with this degree of difficulty. My emphasis on popular culture will account, I believe, for some key elements of the American reception of the Holocaust; I am aware that other approaches will

Preface

explain others. Yet however much variability there may be among these accounts, one conclusion will be inescapable: that the career of the Holocaust in America is an American story.

Chapter 2, "Two Models in the Study of Holocaust Culture," steps back from the task of laying out the American narrative to offer theoretical reflections on what it means to take context seriously. The chapter presents and assesses two contrasting models for the study of cultural responses to the Holocaust generally, and not just in America. The exceptionalist model is based on a conception of the Holocaust as an unprecedented event that transformed our understanding of the world and produced a literature that can be understood only internally and by reference to itself. The constructivist model emphasizes the cultural lens through which the Holocaust is perceived. Even though philosophers and theologians may view the Holocaust as a world-transforming event, the cultural systems of particular societies are slow to absorb such an event and do so only within the terms of that particular culture. The memory of the Holocaust will be shaped differently in Israel, Poland, Germany, France, and America because of the different issues and preoccupations of those cultures before the war. To make the differences between these two positions more concrete, I contrast two important anthologies of Holocaust literature: Lawrence Langer's *Art from the Ashes* as an example of the exceptionalist model and David Roskies's *The Literature of Destruction* as an example of the constructivist model. What is at stake in privileging one of these over the other, I submit, is a series of crucial determinations: Should the ghettos receive as much attention as the concentration camps? Is the model of the survivor narrative brokenness or continuity? Should the Holocaust be the object of a separate branch of academic study? What is the place of the Holocaust in museum presentations of the experience of the Jewish people in modern times?

Chapter 3, "The Holocaust at the Movies," engages the question of the Holocaust and popular culture by offering reception studies of three selected motion pictures: *Judgment at Nuremberg* (1961), *The*

Preface

Pawnbroker (1965), and *Schindler's List* (1993). I stress the fact of selection, because, even though I believe these films to be most important movies on the subject made in Hollywood, a full film history of the Holocaust would adduce many other instances that would locate the singularity of these three films. I also stress that these are studies in reception, which means that they examine how critics and audiences responded to the films and how they understood them. I have not set myself to work within the canons of film studies, film history, and film criticism. My goal instead has been to look at what the reactions to these films reveal about the place of the Holocaust in the American mind and how in turn they shape those conceptions. I have been particularly fascinated by the gap between the reception of the two earlier films when they first appeared in the sixties and retrospective evaluations of them from the "Holocaust consciousness" closer to our own times. As a window into the process whereby the Holocaust has been appropriated in American culture, Hollywood movies are particularly luminous. But there are surely other cultural expressions that would illuminate this process from other vantage points: William Styron's *Sophie's Choice* (especially the book but also the movie), Art Spiegelman's *Maus,* Philip Roth's *The Ghost Writer,* and Cynthia Ozick's *The Shawl.* While reception studies of these works would certainly be welcome, they would have lengthened the book beyond the format of brief studies in which the present volume appears. In the studies of these three films I hope I have laid down a method that can be usefully applied more widely.

The concluding chapter, "The Future of Memorialization," turns from the task of description and analysis to a meditation on how Americans will shape the memory of the Holocaust in the future. Because the Holocaust has been so much in the forefront of public discussion and media treatment it has been difficult to think in longer-range terms about the role this event will play in American culture and in the very different communities that make up our society. One can already observe within the American Jewish community a growing critique of the "preoccupation" with the Holocaust

Preface

and the resulting marginalization of more substantive modes of Jewish experience and commitment. I attempt to present a conceptual framework for thinking about the way in which identification with the Holocaust is wrapped around other motivations; and I go on to give examples of how different "communities of interpretation" in America might go about the task of giving purposeful consideration to the future of Holocaust memory in accordance with their special values and needs. The volume concludes with observations on the possibilities and limitations of what is emerging as the major resource for the shaping of Holocaust memory: videotaped survivor testimony.

The impetus for this study came from an invitation to give the Stroum Lectures at the University of Washington in the spring of 1996. I was deeply honored to be asked to participate in a series that has succeeded in eliciting the best original work of scholars in Jewish studies, and I hope that my contribution will not dim that luster. The hospitality I received in Seattle was exemplary, and I am grateful to Hillel Kieval (now of Washington University in St Louis), Robert Stacey, and Naomi Sokoloff, and of course to the generosity and geniality of Sam and Althea Stroum. The time needed to turn the lectures into a book was enabled by a grant from the Bradley Foundation of Milwaukee, and I am profoundly grateful to Hillel Fradkin and the foundation for this most precious gift. I also thank the provost and the dean of Brandeis University as well as the Department of Near Eastern and Judaic Studies for allowing me to take a leave from my teaching duties to make use of this opportunity.

The role of the Holocaust in American culture is so unstable and multisided a topic that my perspective could have been shaped only through extensive discussions with colleagues, and my gratitude is extended to those who took an interest in my work and share their ideas with me: Michael Berenbaum, Sylvia Barak Fishman, Sara Horowitz, Anthony Polonsky, D. G. Myers, Marcia Pally, Alvin Rosenfeld, Alex Sagan, Jeffrey Shandler, Susan Shapiro and James Young. Rona Sheramy helped me with the research and contributed

Preface

to the spirit of the inquiry. Although Lawrence Langer and I differ on a number of issues, the passionate intellectual clarity and integrity of his work have been a model for me.

I am grateful to the Jewish Theological Seminary and to its library for its hospitality to me as a visiting scholar. I had the privilege of directing summer seminars sponsored by the National Endowment for the Humanities in 1996 and 1999, and I thank the participants in those seminars for many illuminating discussions, the fruits of which they will recognize in these pages. I thank my wife, Susanna Morgenthau, for helping to make this project proceed amid the hectic routines of family life, and my daughters, Amira and Avital, for asking their father each night how many pages he wrote that day.

My greatest debt is to David Roskies, whose commitment to interpret the vital inner world of East European Jews remains the most eloquent testament to both their lives and their deaths.

Popular Culture and the Shaping of Holocaust Memory in America

I

From Silence to Salience

In the depths of the 1940s and 1950s, at a time when the term *Holocaust* as we now use it had not been invented, when survivors were silent and stigmatized, and when the destruction of European Jewry did not figure in public discourse, who could have predicted that the Holocaust would move so forcefully to the center of American culture? Today the Holocaust is pervasive. Every year sees the creation of new museums and research centers devoted to the Holocaust. Many states mandate the teaching of the Holocaust in the schools, university courses on the subject abound, and academic chairs devoted to the new discipline of Holocaust Studies are being established. Tens of thousands of Americans, especially young people, undertake "marches" and "pilgrimages" to Europe to visit the sites of the concentration camps. One cannot enter a serious bookshop without confronting hundreds of titles relating to the Holocaust, whether works of historical research, albums of photographs, or memoirs by survivors. Survivors have become sought-after authorities, even culture heroes. Their stories are told not only in books but aloud before respectful audiences on special days of remembrance. Vast projects have been undertaken to interview survivors on videotape before their testimony is no longer available. The Holocaust has also been admitted into the mainstream media and become the subject of profitable and high-profile film and television projects.

Yet nowhere is the arrival of the Holocaust at center stage in America more dramatically marked than by the museum on the Mall. There, at the monumental core of the republic, established by presidential commission and maintained by congressional subvention, stands a memorial to an event that took place far from native shores. Perhaps the strongest evidence of the Americanization of the Holocaust is represented by the throngs of high school students from all over the land who pass through the United States Holocaust Memorial Museum each and every day and who never seem to pause to consider whether there is anything anomalous about a government-sponsored memorial to the death of European Jewry. They cannot imagine a time in which the remembrance of the Holocaust was not a central American concern. It is taken for granted.

The shift from silence to salience is surely one of the most stunning developments in American culture in our time. Accounting for this shift presents a considerable challenge to the historian that spreads across many networks of explanation and causation. This is a challenge that is just now beginning to be met in several quarters. What I offer in this chapter is not the report of a professional historian with the requisite arsenal of documentary evidence. I offer instead a broad and synthetic account of this movement, and I present it as an interpretation that attempts to gather the manifold strands of explanation into a coherent narrative. My account stresses the pivotal role of works of popular culture in propelling the Holocaust from being a proprietary concern of American Jews to becoming an object of remembrance for the American nation as a whole.[1]

I begin my account by recalling the enormous power of the concept of victory at the end of World War II. At a huge cost and with an outcome that was never assured, America and its allies had vanquished Fascism and liberated its victims from the Nazi beast. Many had died during the war, including American servicemen, and the particular sufferings of European Jews were folded into the general sum of misery and horror that was so widely shared. For a brief moment immediately after the war, graphic newsreel footage taken by U.S. Signal Corps photographers when the army units liberated the camps was shown in American movie houses. But soon afterward, the murder of European Jewry was consigned to the category of evils that had been decisively crushed by the American victory. Like other groups, American Jews participated patriotically in the war effort and, at its conclusion, memorialized their war dead and honored the returning veterans. Individual families, to be sure, grieved privately for European relatives, the true nature of whose tragic fate could only be dimly known. Yet in the public arena, Jews joined fully in celebrating the "Victory," which, like the war effort itself, drew many Americans, especially the sons and daughters of recent immigrants, into a shared experience of the mystique of the American nation.[2]

This was a celebration at which the Holocaust and everything we now associate with it were not welcome guests. Victory over the enemy, embraced as a final and all-encompassing notion, left no room for a tragedy that is unremitting. The enormity of the catastrophe— what it meant for Jews and for the world that a third of the Jewish people had been murdered—simply could not be accommodated by ideas of victory or liberation, no matter what shocking facts may have been available by the end of the war. So this dark and unwanted knowledge was left aside until much later. American outrage over the genocidal atrocities committed by the Germans was short-lived. Interest ebbed after the first round of war crimes trials, as American concern shifted to the threat posed by the ambitions of its former ally the Soviet Union. The question of German guilt was bracketed while the United States rebuilt West Germany and rehabilitated its citizens as a key bulwark against Communist aggression.

In the meantime, American Jews were enthusiastically seizing the new opportunities that opened up to them after the war. Discriminatory bars preventing Jews from enrolling in prestigious universities were eased, and GI benefits afforded the means to do so. Jews were more freely able to enter the liberal professions, and they gained access to the worlds of technology and engineering and even, to some degree, the echelons of corporate management. With increased achievement came greater prosperity. Jews left the ethnic neighborhoods in city centers for the suburbs, where they built not only homes but large synagogues and community centers. This transformation fundamentally changed the way Jews and Judaism were perceived in America. Judaism became an American religion. From being seen as members of an ethnic group, like the Irish or the Italians, Jews began to be thought of as Americans who, like Protestants and Catholics, adhere to one of America's three great faiths.

Some Jews used this new openness to seek absorption into the general culture and to distance themselves from their Jewish origins, to the degree that a residually Christian America would allow them to do so. Many others participated broadly in American culture while retaining elements of their ethnic and religious identities. Yet whether they chose the path of radical assimilation or more adaptive acculturation, for American Jews this forceful move into the mainstream of American life was not accomplished without anxiety or an enormous mobilization of social energies. An acute awareness of the Holocaust was not part of the American Jewish experience during the first two decades after the event because it impeded this process of Americanization in two ways. Like all immigrant groups entering the mainstream, Jews sought to avoid distinctiveness in the public sphere, however much they held onto their own ways privately. Overt identification with the Holocaust and memorialization of its victims would have drawn unwanted notice at a time when Americans were united in their pride over the complete vanquishing of Nazism. Furthermore, admitting the full horror of the Holocaust would have placed an unbearable demand upon the disciplined energies necessary to take advantage of the unparalleled opportunities then being offered to American Jews.

The reticence of American Jews to draw attention to the Holocaust during these years is most often ascribed—mistakenly, to my mind—to the effects of trauma.[3] The community was traumatized by the destruction of European Jewry and went into prolonged denial, according to this explanation. So raw was the unconscious grief that it required a significant passage of time before the loss could be openly mourned and the tragedy directly engaged. Now, this account may describe the situation of some families who lost close relatives in the war. But for the generality of American Jews it would be fair to say that the avoidance of the Holocaust took place outside the cycle of denial and grief rather than inside it. Jews were too deeply engaged in the energetic enterprise of entering American society and seizing the opportunities offered to them to be available to the subversive sadness provoked by the Holocaust. It was not until this project was complete and Jews felt more at ease in America as Americans and, moreover, the luster of America itself had dimmed, that American Jews were ready for this dark encounter.

The parallel to what was happening at this time in Israeli society is well worth noting. For all the vast differences between the situation of American Jews in the lap of postwar prosperity and liberty and the situation of Israeli Jews in the grip of austerity and military vulnerability, there remains a remarkably similar public avoidance of discussing the destruction of European Jewry and, I would argue, for similar reasons.[4] Just as American Jews threw themselves into building their lives and improving their lots on these shores, so Israeli Jews threw themselves into facing the challenges of building and defending the new Jewish state. The tasks may be very different, but the kind of totalization required for each is similar. In both cases, moreover, distance from the Holocaust was given a forceful ideological charge. For American Jews, the overwhelming appeal of Americanization attenuated the connection to the Old Country to the point of a feeble nostalgia or an embarrassed contempt. For Israelis, the heroic and pioneering ideals of Zionism had long ago detached them from the benighted and exilic impotence of East European Jewry.

The identification with the struggles of the new state of Israel provides an instructive exception to American Jews' avoidance of distinctiveness. American Jews, both individually and through various institutions and agencies, were active to varying degrees in lobbying for American support for Israel and in providing direct assistance. On the one hand, identifying with the murdered Jews of Europe, which was difficult on many counts, elicited an unwanted sense of vulnerability and victimhood at a time when Jews were gratified by the recent retreat of anti-Semitism in America. (It was just this sense of victimhood that would change its moral valence in the identity politics of the eighties and nineties, when Jews were eager to identify themselves as the belated bearers of a greater burden of historical suffering than other groups in America.[5]) Identifying with the brave farmer-soldiers of Israel, on the other hand, was another matter. The state rose from the ashes of the Holocaust and courageously and at great cost gathered in the remnants of European Jewry and the vulnerable Jewries in Arab lands. This was an image that was ennobling and energizing rather than shameful and dispiriting, and if it made American Jews more visible as Jews, it also allied them with the American admiration for the pluck of the underdog.

For the survivors who arrived in America after the war—as well as in a proximate sense for the refugees who gained entry just before—the situation was obviously different, but not in ways that were unaffected by the American ethos of the forties and fifties. They themselves were greatly absorbed in the challenges of recreating families, learning English, making a living, and generally becoming established in America. Telling the story of what had happened to them and to those who had not survived, was not something survivors often chose to do even in the family circle, not to mention in public settings. In the Jewish community and American society at large, moreover, there was little receptivity to such testimony. Survivors themselves were often not held in high esteem but rather viewed as morally tainted by the ordeal they had been forced to undergo. The very term *survivor,* with its intimation of heroism, did not come into wide currency until much later. During these years, the former victims of Nazism were called refugees, a term that minimizes the extremity of their fate and vaguely lumps them together with immigrants and exiles and other foreigners who have sought and found refuge on American shores. Survivors socialized among themselves and formed societies for mutual aid and memorialization, but intercourse with the wider American Jewish community remained limited. There was no invitation offered to draw closer and speak of what had happened "over there."

For the very Orthodox among the survivors, especially the remnants of the lost worlds of Hungarian Hasidism and the Lithuanian yeshivot, America also provided a set of opportunities. Energetic and charismatic religious leaders who had been rescued or had survived on their own saw in America a safe haven in which institutions of worship and study, which had already long been in decline in Europe, could be bolstered and rebuilt. The emphasis was placed on establishing large families to repopulate the religious world and creating schools and academies in which the study of Torah could be widely made into an object of prestige and preeminence. Despite the seductions of the modern American consumer culture, America offered constitutional protections for the practice of religion, restraints against persecution, and the prospect of material prosperity. The troubling theological mysteries raised by the destruction of European Jewry were not dwelt on. The answer to Hitler, it was asserted, was more babies and more yeshivot rather than more testimony and reflection. Like their less religious counterparts in the wider Jewish community, who were preoccupied with becoming Americans, the very Orthodox were too busy moving in their own directions to speak of the Holocaust.

How and when was this avoidance of confronting the Holocaust, shared across so many sectors of American Jewry, overcome? How and when did the Holocaust become not just a special concern of the Jewish community but a focus of attention for the American nation as a whole? This is truly an enormous shift and the reasons for it are many. There are key events, for example, that serve as mark-

From Silence to Salience

ers of the change: *The Diary of Anne Frank* in its film and stage versions, the Eichmann trial, the Six-Day War, the 1978 television miniseries *Holocaust,* the founding of the U.S. Holocaust Memorial Museum. There are also broad and deep changes in consciousness and social forces that permitted the Holocaust to move from the margins to the center.

A key factor, to begin with, was a shift in the very conception of America as a paragon society. Together with other Americans at midcentury, the sons and daughters of immigrants held the United States to be the most glorious country on earth; it was the freest and most just, in addition to being the richest and most powerful. To camouflage one's distinctiveness in order to be fully counted in such a society did not seem like an unworthy renunciation. Yet with the advent of the civil rights movement and the war in Vietnam, the meaning of America became more complicated. The critique of the justness of American society and its use of power opened up the prospect of seeing America not as a shining example to the world but as a country that caused suffering at home and abroad. A growing awareness of the catastrophic consequences of "man's inhumanity to man" was epitomized by the hopelessness of the black underclass in the inner cities and by the burned flesh and torn limbs of Vietnamese peasants. In this context, it is not surprising, then, that the Holocaust eventually became the ultimate analogy for reflecting on the evils humans have afflicted upon other humans. The urban quarters in which the poor were concentrated were called ghettos, the attempt of a strong nation to destroy a minority within its midst was called genocide, and the prospect of a conflict using atomic weapons was called a nuclear holocaust. Upon the Jews was conferred the dubious moral prestige of being the ultimate victims of historical evil.

In the present, however, and in the immediacy of the American context, it was African-Americans who claimed this distinction for themselves. The partnership between blacks and liberal Jews, which had been based on a universalization of Jewish values and a common history of oppression, broke down as more militant civil rights leaders took the movement in nationalist and separatist directions. This was a signal moment in the history of American society in which the notion of a single nation containing Americans from different backgrounds was severely challenged. Distinctiveness and difference were suddenly being emphatically asserted in many quarters rather than muffled. Jews who had been involuntarily separated from the civil rights movement and many others who had been sympathetic onlookers were forced back upon their Jewishness by the strident "identity politics" of the 1960s. Internal constraints on the public expression of Jewishness and on the inquiry into the meaning of Jewish tradition and Jewish historical experience began to be lifted.

A crucial event was the capture and trial of Adolf Eichmann in 1960–61. What was intended by Ben-Gurion as a public demonstration of Israel's pluck and its leadership of the world Jewish people turned into a much more complex event. For many Americans, Jews and non-Jews alike, the Jerusalem trial, which was reported and broadcast around the world, was the first time they grasped the full story of the murder of European Jewry. The trial took place at a critical juncture at which there emerged a greater willingness to accept realities that had existed on record but had been kept at a distance. Although the grim facts had long been available for those who cared to know them, it was only as a result of the trial that names and places and numbers were turned into visceral knowledge. The case presented by the prosecution, moreover, amounted to an epic retelling of the Holocaust narrative. The Nuremberg Laws, the ghettos, the deportations, the mobile killing units on the Eastern Front, the Final Solution, the mechanics of the death camps, the forced marches—the whole, colossal Nazi effort to liquidate the Jews was laid out for the world to see in vivid and systematic detail.

The intensely public nature of the trial not only communicated an enormous amount of information; it also transformed the status of the Holocaust in the American mind. It became, in a sense, "registered" in American collective memory as a key event in the modern age and as a watershed in the definition of what humanity is capable of. Although the Holocaust in no way replaced the great patriotic American narrative of "WWII," a niche was created alongside that chronicle to make room for this other story that had no uplifting ending. The recognition of the Holocaust by the gentile world, moreover, had an important impact on the Jews. The modest stream of documentation and memorialization of the Holocaust before the trial had been produced by a small number of devoted Jewish historians and survivors. The heightened moral status now accorded the Holocaust in the larger world had the effect for American Jews of encouraging them—actually, giving them license—to pay more attention to this aspect of their own past and make it the object of broad and intense inquiry.

The trial also placed the Holocaust on the moral screen of the Christian community in America. The record of the major European churches regarding the Jews during the war ranged from the ignoble to the equivocal, with scattered acts of moral heroism. The high visibility of the trial prompted renewed scrutiny, from both within and without the church, concerning Christian responsibility and collaboration. Public discussion was quickened a few years later by Rolf Hochhuth's play *The Deputy,* which raised troubling questions about relations between the Vatican and the Third Reich. Yet beyond the stimulus to contrition and self-scourging created by the trial, there emerged, more importantly, an opportunity for a positive theological connection to the Jews. The exorbitant and multilayered sufferings of the Jewish victims in the ghettos and the camps created a space of affliction and torment that was familiar to the Christian imagination. While it may have been difficult in the past to sustain an admiration for the mix of mercantile achievement, textual erudition, and punctilious observance of the law that characterized traditional Jewish life in the Diaspora, it was considerably easier to revere the Jews in the throes of their martyrdom. The passion of the Jews in the Holocaust made them more compelling to Christian thought than at any time in the past since the emergence of Christianity from rabbinic Judaism. The Jews had again become an active and relevant presence in the Christian mind in America.

The status of the survivors was also greatly enhanced through the deliberations of the trial. The survivors appeared in the Jerusalem courtroom in a new role: not as victims but as expert witnesses with crucial testimony to offer. Rather than being a shameful tale better left untold, the record of the torments they had been forced to endure was turned into a source of privileged knowledge that was their duty to divulge to the world. The experience was undoubtedly cathartic for the small number of witnesses who testified at the trial; for survivors around the world the impact had an even stronger resonance. For the first time, survivors came to be viewed by others and by themselves as the possessors of a special aura derived from the authority of their experience; and, for the first time, they felt that an invitation was being extended to come forward and tell their stories. In many cases, however, the stories were not ready-made and waiting to be told. The long suppression of survivors' voices had affected the ability to retrieve, articulate, and shape the internal narrative. Reclaiming one's experience by voicing it first to oneself and then to others was a process that began at this time and reached its apotheosis later on with the emergence of the survivor as hero, whose story became a master narrative of our times.

The single greatest factor shaping the perception of the victims and the survivors of the Holocaust was the question of passivity and collaboration. There was a widespread presumption, implied if unspoken, that Jews had gone to their deaths "like sheep to the slaughter" and that their blinkered innocence had been tantamount to collusion with the Nazi perpetrators. It was felt that if this in fact was the truth about Jewish behavior during these dark times, then it was a truth that was better not publicly rehearsed. The testimony of historians and survivors at the trial did a great deal to recast this perceived truth. The revision took place not through the deliberate presentation of counterevidence and counterarguments but rather simply through the issue being brought into the open and the procedures of the Nazi campaign against the Jews rendered in detail. Understanding the complexity of what actually happened to the victims, especially the tactic of collective reprisals, and hearing the accounts of those who actually experienced the horror acted as critical antidotes to a widespread avoidance rooted in shame and judgment. Paradoxically, the most judgmental and best-known account of the trial, Hannah Arendt's *Eichmann in Jerusalem* (written originally as a series of reports for the *New Yorker*), had the effect of provoking many, especially Jewish intellectuals who had been distant from Jewish issues, into a better-informed and more empathic connection to the Holocaust and its victims and survivors.

Six years after the Eichmann trial, the shock of the Six-Day War provided a catalyst for a new constellation of Jewish attitudes toward heroism and passivity. Since the beginning of the century there had always been a significant but circumscribed Zionist movement in America, which, in its established forms, had stressed the need for a Jewish homeland in Palestine as a haven for persecuted European Jewry rather than as a magnet for emigration from America. The struggle for independence in the face of the Arab onslaught was understood against the background of the Holocaust, as portrayed in Leon Uris's enormously popular 1958 novel, *Exodus* (Otto Preminger's film version appeared in 1960). In the 1950s there was a widespread "Zionization" of American Jewry. Jewish organizations that had stood aloof from the Zionist movement now joined a broad communal consensus that affirmed the importance of the new state. Among the rank and file of American Jewry, Israel enjoyed a high degree of acceptance; American Jews were proud of Israel's victory and found much vicarious romantic fulfillment in the courageous image of the Israeli citizen soldier-farmer. This was a fulfillment that could be enjoyed with little risk or sacrifice; in return for the fortifying of their pride very little was asked of American Jews beyond financial support. Israel's public success in the world arena, moreover, served as a counter to the private shame induced by memories of more equivocal Jewish behavior during the Holocaust.

The threat to Israel's existence in the weeks preceding the Six-Day War was also a threat to the vicariously achieved security of American Jews. The life-and-death threat to Israel presented itself, to be sure, on an entirely different level of seriousness than the ordeals of identity and distinctiveness experienced by American Jews. Yet within the terms of Jewish life in America, the crisis was a real one. Impotent, imperfectly informed, and uncertain about raising its voice, American Jewry had stood by in the 1940s while the Jews of Europe were slaughtered. Now a quarter of a century later, in full possession of the facts and in full awareness of the stakes, American Jews looked on again at the possibility that a whole segment of the Jewish people would be destroyed.

This time American Jewry did mobilize itself in a remarkable show of financial and political assistance. But the outpouring of support for Israel masked the gravity of a drama that was unfolding within the American community. It took a crisis of this severity to make many positively identifying American Jews acknowledge to themselves how deeply connected they were to Israel and its achievements and how dependent were their identities as Jews on the continued success of the Zionist enterprise. For others, Jews who were more deeply assimilated into the American milieu and intellectuals who had distanced themselves from their particularistic origins, the war had the effect of a slap in the face that reawakened an awareness of past choices that now deserved reconsideration. By virtue of the actions on the world stage taken by their Israeli counterparts, American Jews could no longer avoid—nor did they wish to—the distinctiveness they had sought for so long to elude.

Israel's lightning victory *during* the war had a confirming effect upon the cathartic affirmations made on the *eve* of the war. This time the prospect of catastrophe without its dread fulfillment was enough to stir the conscience. In all this reawakening of identity, the specter of the Holocaust hovered continually in the background, and not simply as a ghostly presence or a metaphor. The actuality of the Holocaust became the standard of horror against which the alarm of the present hour was to be measured, and as such, it moved into the conscious awareness of a widening circle of American Jews.

But what of American *non*-Jews? As a tiny minority of the American population, Jews might be expected to be concerned with the fate of their brethren past and present, although, as we have seen, that concern was not automatically forthcoming. Yet for the vast reaches of the American people, especially those who did not live near large Jewish communities, there was little inherent reason why the Holocaust should be perceived as an event inscribed within their radius of concern. It was, after all, an event that had taken place far from American shores, and it was a secondary drama in a war that had claimed the lives of multitudes of servicemen whose loss was felt much closer to home. More important, the matter was over and done with and, as such, joined the long record of benighted human misery that belonged to the Old World. With so much suffering spread so widely around the world, why *should* Americans, in fact, give special attention to this particular instance? True, there would always be here and there some individuals of conscience, students of history and sensitive churchmen, who would display an awareness of the dimensions and significance of the catastrophe. Yet for the great majority of Americans, the event had remained only a distant echo. In time, however, changes began to occur. Important sectors of the American public did come to view the Holocaust as an issue that belongs on the American agenda, and wheels were set in motion that eventually brought about the creation of the Washington museum and other broadly supported sites of memorialization.

How the Holocaust succeeded in penetrating layers of American isolationism is not a simple matter. The key to this question, I believe, lies in the power of cultural texts and their diffusion in the form of books, stage plays, movies, and television. The image of Anne Frank, in the various media in which it was refracted, is the chief example of a process that continued to unfold in various Hollywood movies, the 1978 TV miniseries *Holocaust,* and more recently, *Schindler's List.*[6]

The publication of the English translation of Anne Frank's *The Diary of a Young Girl* in 1952, nine years before the Eichmann trial, was a signal event whose impact upon the awareness of the Holocaust cannot be overestimated. The power of the diary lay in its ability to do what no political event had done: to create a bridge of empathic connection, even identification, between the fate of European Jewry and ordinary American readers who had no ethnic or religious link to the victims and often no knowledge whatsoever of the event itself. The diary succeeded in overcoming the natural American resistance to reading about unhappy things because it steered clear of the horror and because it stressed the commonality of human experience rather than the distinctiveness of the victims. Although Anne's life ended in the camps, the setting of her diary is a recognizable domestic space that, however constrained and clandestine, exists alongside the world of atrocity rather than within it. The family life that takes place within the "secret annex" is approachable in its familiarity. For although the Franks are German Jews who have recently emigrated to the Netherlands and are instantly recognizable as such to their Dutch neighbors, they are acculturated Jews in whose daily lives the rituals and practices of Judaism play little role. For the American reader, their Jewishness is more an invisible fate than a matter of substance that would interpose itself as a unsettling foreignness.

The attractiveness of Anne herself is undoubtedly the diary's most potent charm. Her passion and pluck are balanced by her knowing observations of herself and the others in her small circle. Her wish to become a writer comes across not as an adolescent enthusiasm but as a focused aspiration that is richly validated by the finely honed quality of her prose. Although her diary is a kind of writer's exercise book, it clearly indicates that she would have become a major writer had she lived; and it is the unsentimental, "writerly" quality of her narrative that makes the account of adolescence so affecting.

From Silence to Salience

What she reveals about herself is, in the end, the stuff of adolescent exuberance and turmoil everywhere and always: the need for love, the confusions of puberty, the budding interest in boys, the ambitions for the future, the skirmishes with parents, the misunderstandings and self-dramatizations. That these ordinary stirrings of youth should take place under conditions of life-and-death uncertainty gives the diary its pathos, but it is the resolutely ordinary quality of those stirrings that makes the empathic connection possible.

The diary is an extraordinary document; the story of how the image of Anne was fashioned after her death is more extraordinary still. Even before the diary was published, there was already a move to make the figure of Anne even more appealing than she already was. Her father, Otto Frank, went through the manuscript and excised passages that made too explicit references to sexuality or that excoriated Anne's mother for her lack of empathy and other failings in her daughter's eyes. The major revision came when the English translation of the diary, published with a foreword by Eleanor Roosevelt, was made into a Broadway play (1956) and Hollywood movie (1959), both of which were enormously successful and treated as major events in American cultural life.

The question of who would get to write the stage play, to begin with, was highly contested. Meyer Levin, a Jewish journalist who had been an early champion of the diary, lost out to the non-Jewish Hollywood-based husband-and-wife team Albert Hackett and Frances Goodrich, who had done many previous successful adaptations. Their refashioning of the diary, which also set the tone for the film version, is remarkable for two reasons. Anne's Jewishness is considerably downplayed. Despite the acculturation of the family, Anne's diary entries in fact unambiguously affirm her identity as a member of the Jewish people and display an acute awareness of her situation as a Jew in Nazi Europe in relationship to historical anti-Semitism. In the play, however, her Jewishness is not hidden but made to seem inessential; her identity is folded into the generality of victims of fascism and even into the larger class of the unjust sufferers of the world.

From Silence to Salience

The second change had to do with Anne's optimism and her generosity toward humanity. Anne is a young person with a hopeful nature. Although she is annoyed at the shortcomings of her family members and the others with whom she must live cheek-by-jowl, she understands the frailties of human nature under such conditions. She believes in the essential goodness of the Dutch people and in the compassion of its royal house. While she comprehends the darkness of Jewish fate in the present moment, the unspeakable horrors of the concentrationary universe, which sadly she will come to know later on, lie beyond her grasp within the boundaries of the diary. It is the stunning arrogation of the stage and film versions to take this hopefulness, epitomized in the statement "In spite of all, I still believe men are good" and transpose it from the diary, written before she experienced the reality of Auschwitz and Bergen-Belsen, to the closing scene of the drama, which ends with her death in the camps and with the doubly inspiring implication that Anne's affirmation holds true even after all she has seen and endured. There has been considerable controversy, beginning with Meyer Levin's polemics and litigation, concerning the motives of the writers and the producers in making this change and all of the other selective emphases reflected in the play. It has been argued that the fault lies in part with the involvement of the influential playwright Lillian Hellman, whose fellow-traveling sympathies sought to de-Judaize Anne so that she might serve as a shining example of the common front against fascism. Even without this political calculation, it is evident that all concerned in bringing the diary to stage and screen were focused on the single goal of removing obstacles that might impede a direct emotional connection with the figure of Anne. Whatever objections can be made to their "version" of the diary—and there are many grounds for objection—it is indisputable that Goodrich and Hackett knew their audience and its threshold of revulsion and that they accomplished their goal with enormous success.[7]

The ardent response to the story of another adolescent, whose Holocaust memoir is rawer and more troubling than Anne's, indi-

cates how the tolerance of the audience increased in the years following the publication of the diary. The Jewishness of the narrator
of Elie Wiesel's *Night,* which appeared in English in 1960, is of an
entirely different order than that of Otto Frank and his family. The
autobiographical narrator is a young talmudist with an interest in
Jewish mystical teachings growing up in a Jewish town in Transylvania.
The site of the memoir is vastly different as well. After describing
a brief period of occupation and ghettoization, the narrative moves
squarely into the dark world of Auschwitz with all the appurtenances
of atrocity that were later to become familiar to readers of Holocaust
literature. Nevertheless, there are a number of critical mediations
that enabled general readers, who had not yet been exposed to the
revelations of the Eichmann trial—although that was to come very
soon—to assimilate the enormity of the news being presented to
them. This begins with an act of self-censorship and self-revision on
Wiesel's part. *Night* is an English translation of the French original,
La Nuit, which was published in 1958 and written by Wiesel while
he worked as a journalist in Paris. The French text is itself based on
an earlier work of Wiesel's in Yiddish, *Un di velt hot geshvigen (And
the World Was Silent),* which was considerably longer and which
denounced the gentile nations for standing by during the slaughter
of European Jewry. The process of reworking his Yiddish text into
a French narrative was in part a matter of a young writer's learning
to edit himself and accommodate the French canons of good writing that stressed brevity and restraint. But it was also a process—
which took place under the tutelage of the eminent writer François
Mauriac, who wrote an influential foreword to the French text—
which involved containing the Jewish rage expressed in the Yiddish
and emphasizing the Job-like suffering of the individual human soul.[8]

In contrast to the thick analytic description offered by Primo Levi,
the world of the camps in *Night* is presented as a series of lyric, tele-
graphic mise-en-scènes that focus the reader's attention on the theological and existential ordeals at the center of the narrative. God
fails the young narrator when he is forced to witness the hanging of

From Silence to Salience

an angelic youth. The death of God the Father is linked to the enfeeblement and demoralization of the narrator's own father. Within minutes of arrival at Auschwitz, the narrator is stripped of his mother and sisters, who are taken to be gassed, and is left to face the struggle for survival with his father alone. A remote man, formerly involved more in the affairs of the community than in the lives of his children, the father now becomes the son's burden; the narrator's consciousness becomes consumed by the vicissitudes of the reversal of the relationship, in which the son now has to fight hopelessly to protect the father. The universality of Wiesel's themes, the failure of God and the failure of the father, made *Night* a powerful text for an audience that was becoming more knowledgeable about the Holocaust and that was ready to follow Wiesel's autobiographical narrator into the dark domain that Anne Frank had also entered in her life but not in her diary. As books, *The Diary of a Young Girl* and *Night* had similar careers; exalted by intellectuals as revelations when they originally appeared, these works gradually became classics for younger readers as a first point of contact with the Holocaust.

The fact that Wiesel survived and Anne Frank did not enabled the growing moral prestige associated with survivorhood to attach itself to a living person who could continue to write and reflect on his ordeal. Wiesel continued to write about the Holocaust, but instead of returning to the harrowing world of the camps, his fiction after *Night* explored the inner world of the survivors more than that of the victims and pursued the meaning of the Holocaust in terms that were increasingly symbolic and fabulistic. Wiesel devoted much of his energy to presenting to contemporary audiences the wealth of Jewish legends taken from the Hebrew Bible, rabbinic midrash, and the Hasidic masters and to retelling these stories in a way that reflects an awareness of the events of recent history. Wiesel used the special status he had achieved to speak out on public issues of conscience relating to the security of Israel, the struggles of Soviet Jewry, and the memorialization of the Holocaust, and he soon became the unofficial moral spokesman of the American Jewish community. The extending of the issues he addressed to the international arena brought him the Nobel Peace Prize in 1986.

Wiesel's rise to prominence on the world scene was part of a broader reevaluation of the survivor's moral and cultural status in American society, and not the survivor of the Holocaust alone. The Stalinist legacy in the Soviet Union had succeeded Nazi Germany in the American mind as the embodiment of evil. In their determination to persist in their humanity, the prisoners of the Gulag described in the works of Aleksandr Solzhenitsyn achieved a heroic status that outstrips the massive forces of the malevolence that had been thrust against them. Sympathy and admiration were extended also to contemporary Soviet dissidents and the Jewish refuseniks, the current victims of the Soviet regime, and to writers and intellectuals exiled from Eastern Block countries. The survivor became one of the most vivid heroic ideals of the age, and Elie Wiesel stood as its chief exemplar. Wiesel's eloquence and visibility gave broad encouragement to Holocaust survivors throughout America to step forward into the public sphere on special days of remembrance and as part of educational programs and to relate the account of their ordeals to increasingly receptive audiences. The stigma attached to survivors had gradually been removed, and in the meantime survivors had succeeded in the hard work of building families and businesses. Now that attitudes had shifted to make their stories sought after, survivors could afford, in several senses, to let memory speak.

Significantly, survivors transcended their role as witnesses and began to assert their authority in the politics of memorialization. There had long been organizations of survivors who had been imprisoned in the same camp or came from the same region. These groups functioned like *landsmanschaften,* societies of mutual assistance, circulating information, holding periodic memorial gatherings, and often compiling *yizkorbikher,* albums of remembrances of destroyed communities. Led by Wiesel's example beginning in the 1970s, this inward-looking activity was supplemented by the demand that the Holocaust be actively memorialized by the main-

From Silence to Salience

stream American Jewish community and even by the people of the United States and its government. A widespread consensus had developed around the need for public remembrance of the Holocaust; the immediacy and moral authority of the survivors' voices often served to spur the initiation of new projects or to quicken the development of plans for museums, memorials, and education centers that had languished in the planning stages or been delayed by conflicting communal politics.

The culmination of this process was the formation in 1978 under President Jimmy Carter of a presidential commission on the memorialization of the Holocaust, which resulted, after many vicissitudes, in the creation of the U.S. Holocaust Memorial Museum on the Mall in Washington, D.C. The story of the museum and its making is a remarkable one on many scores, but no aspect of it is more amazing than the gap it crossed between the Jewish community and the nation as a whole. An awareness of the existence of the Holocaust and its great sufferings, as we have seen, had been slowly diffusing into the general American mind. But awareness and even empathy are not the same as the felt obligation to initiate public acts of remembrance. This was an imperative concerning their own murdered European brethren that the leadership of the American Jewish community came to accept only belatedly. That the American people through the federal government should take on this duty represents the crossing of an important line.

The move from awareness to memorialization was impelled, once again, by the power of a cultural artifact. In 1978 the nine-and-a-half-hour television miniseries *Holocaust* was presented by NBC-TV to an audience of 120 million viewers, 50 percent of the American population, and despite the program's mediocrity on many levels, its impact was huge. The success of Alex Haley's *Roots* in 1977, which had been television's first multipart drama on a serious social theme, prepared the audience for a more sustained engagement with Holocaust themes than it had ever been called upon to undertake. The series is an early example of the "docudrama" genre, which mixes fictional characters and events with historical ones. The fates of the members of the fictional Weiss family, a typical upper-middle-class German Jewish family, are caught up in the implementation of the Final Solution, whose planning is reconstructed in dramatizations of actual Nazi meetings. In contrast to previous media representations like *Judgment at Nuremberg,* the television series forthrightly presents the Holocaust as a Jewish event rather than as a universalized catastrophe in which the Jews were incidentally numbered among the victims. A note of proto-Zionist hopefulness is injected at the end of the drama when one member of the Weiss family survives and joins the resistance. On the whole, however, *Holocaust* does not flinch from presenting extermination as the overwhelming fate of European Jewry.

Although *Holocaust* represented the best commercial television was capable of at the time, it left most serious viewers dissatisfied. There were historical inaccuracies. Telling the story of the Holocaust through the tribulations of one family made the oversimplifications of soap opera conventions inevitable. Many were offended by the presence of commercial interruptions such as advertisements for germ-killing bathroom cleansers interspersed with scenes of Nazis planning to rid the Reich of the Jewish infestation. Among the most vehemently outraged was Elie Wiesel, who attacked the series as a vulgarization of the Holocaust in the pages of the *New York Times;* his attack was widely joined by other critics of the series, who in turn were criticized by its defenders. Like the debate provoked by Hannah Arendt after the Eichmann trial, the controversy occasioned by the airing of *Holocaust* was in its own way as important as the series itself.[9] While the earlier debate focused on issues of passivity and self-defense, this later one shifted the discussion to the problems of the aesthetic representation of the Holocaust and the capacity of popular media such as television to treat the event without trivializing it. The two positions that emerged in the debate surrounding *Holocaust* would later be restated with variations each time a new commercially successful treatment of the Holocaust would come on the scene. One position argued that the vulgarity of a given film or show was mitigated by its power to convey the "message" of the Holocaust to those who would otherwise be untouched by it. The other position argued that any vulgarization of the Holocaust cannot escape betraying the victims and desecrating the sacred mystery of the event.

That the 1978 television series was at least guilty of trivialization was evident to all. But it was not a travesty of the Holocaust. It did succeed in recreating the historical mood of the period and in conveying a considerable amount of information about the Nazi plan to murder Europe's Jews and how it was carried out. After the publication of Robert Morse's *While Six Million Died* in 1967 and Lucy Dawidowicz's *The War against the Jews* in 1976, after the 1973 war in Israel and the Entebbe rescue in 1976 (when Jews had been "selected" from among other prisoners), the American public was ready to have the events of the Holocaust presented in a direct but popularly accessible form. The producer, Herbert Brodkin, and the writer, Gerald Green, chose a story line about an acculturated German Jewish family, much like Anne Frank's family, that was designed to maximize the identification of ordinary American viewers with the victims. Most important, the potential of television was exploited to the fullest. In the words of *Time* magazine's Frank Rich:

> TV's built-in limitations . . . can make difficult material more accessible to a mass audience. It is hard to imagine *Holocaust* being so effective in another format. Were the show exhibited in movie theaters, no one would sit still for its 9 and a 1/2-hour runner time. Were it produced for PBS, Holocaust would probably be drowned in a sea of historical minutiae. By creating their show for NBC, the authors have forced themselves to be equally responsive to the demands of both prime-time show biz and historical accuracy. They prove that such a marriage of commerce and art can bear remarkable fruit.[10]

From Silence to Salience

The success of *Holocaust* represented, in a sense, something even more stunning than the marriage of art and commerce. It represented the intersection of a mass medium that was a quintessentially American invention with a virulent mode of Jewish persecution that was a quintessentially European invention. A catastrophe that had taken place far from the soil of American consciousness had gained admittance through the engine of entertainment that Americans had devised to protect their historical innocence.

Beyond the mass diffusion of information, the television series marked a turning point at which the Holocaust emerged as a moral metaphor of great power in American society. While still "belonging" to the Jews, the Holocaust underwent a process of universalization in two senses. The murder of European Jewry became the ultimate standard for speaking of the victimization of peoples in the modern period in spheres that had no necessary connection to the Jews. The Holocaust had become the referent for collective suffering. In the political arena, the Holocaust became a rarity in American life: a point of moral consensus. A political leader who championed memorialization of the Holocaust could be confident that his actions would be applauded by many and criticized by very few. It was with precisely this confidence that on the thirtieth anniversary of the creation of Israel on May 1, 1978, two weeks after *Holocaust* had been aired on national television, President Jimmy Carter announced the creation of a commission to recommend a national Holocaust memorial. Carter was motivated in part by a need to shore up his relationship to a Jewish community that had become profoundly mistrustful of the president over the Saudi arms deal and his desire to recognize the Palestine Liberation Organization. At the same time, the president professed himself to be deeply affected by a 1963 trip to Israel, by his reading of Arthur Morse's *While Six Million Died,* which he described as "the tragic account of the ultimate in man's inhumanity to man, the Holocaust," and by the awareness that the state of Israel had been born "out of the ashes" of the Holocaust.

The journey from Carter's announcement in the White House

From Silence to Salience

rose garden in 1978 through the Reagan and Bush years into the Clinton presidency when the U.S. Holocaust Memorial Museum opened its doors in 1993 was a rocky one that threatened to break down at many points along the way. The problems had less to do with traditional Washington politics in a narrow sense than with the new "identity politics" in which different ethnic groups in America contended for moral authority and prominence. During the first five years of this process—before the idea of a museum, as opposed to other forms of memorialization, had been adopted—controversy centered on the issue of whether the Jews alone "owned" Holocaust memory or whether its ownership was to be shared with other groups, and, furthermore, to what degree the lessons of the Holocaust should be universalized to include acts of genocide that took place before and after World War II. From the beginning, President Carter spoke about eleven million victims of the Holocaust, of whom six million were Jews and five million were others, including Poles and other Slavs, homosexuals, Gypsies, Christian groups, and political prisoners. Without objecting to the special place of the Jews in the Holocaust, representatives of those groups with large populations in America, especially Polish Americans, sought to be included in the commission and its advisory board and to widen the focus of the memorialization efforts in the planning.

Until he resigned in 1986 as chair of the Holocaust Council (which had succeed the presidential commission), Elie Wiesel was the most aggressive and powerful advocate of the position that the Holocaust was a uniquely Jewish event and that the substantive inclusion of other victims in a memorial would detract from the focus on the eradication of the Jews as the Nazi's chief war aim. Wiesel's allies on the council were other Jewish Holocaust survivors whom he had been instrumental in appointing (such as Hadassah Rosenhaft, Miles Lerman, and Sigmund Strochlitz) and who trusted Wiesel to hold the line against an inclusiveness that would inevitably lead, in their view, to a dilution and contamination of Holocaust memory. The role of the survivors on the council, it should be noted, represented a new stage in the profile of former victims of the Holocaust in America. The survivor members of the council were appointed because of the very fact they were survivors, in addition to their considerable community involvements and business achievements. As survivors, they were able to share in the moral aura created by Wiesel on the strength of their firsthand experience of the event that stood at the center of the council's mandate and about which others could discourse but not speak from a standpoint of personal experience and personal suffering. Their suffering and their survival had made them into sacred witnesses, and their authority could be commanding even when it came to disagreements with museum professionals over the design of the permanent exhibits.

Exerted against Wiesel and the other survivors were a variety of pressures to make the planning process and the museum that would result from it more inclusive and, in a word, more American. It was natural for the administration and Congress to seek to add more members from wider constituencies to the council, just as Wiesel sought to have more survivors appointed to counter the moves toward greater inclusion. The balance of power shifted back and forth. Michael Berenbaum, a close associate and disciple of Wiesel's, resigned from the directorship of the commission in 1980, over Wiesel's refusal to accommodate the American political context necessary for any memorial or museum to be realized. In 1986 Wiesel resigned as chair of the council out of the conviction that the uniqueness of Jewish Holocaust memory had been too far compromised. In 1987 Berenbaum was brought back to become project director for the planning of the museum and eventually became head of the museum's research institute. It was Berenbaum's achievement to formulate and broker the way in which an exclusivist definition of the Jewish Holocaust could make room for gestures of inclusion relating to the persecution of other groups. Berenbaum argued that the uniqueness of Jewish experience in the Holocaust was not diminished by the inclusion of other victims of Nazism but in fact enhanced by making the Jewish catastrophe into a universal point of reference

From Silence to Salience

for all victims of genocidal persecution. It is Berenbaum's formulation, which places the Jews at the center of the conception of the Holocaust but includes others among the victims, that became the basis for the narrative of the Holocaust told in the museum's permanent installation.

Wiesel's resignation further signaled an essential discomfort with the very idea of a museum rather than a memorial. As demonstrated in his censure of the television series *Holocaust,* Wiesel is profoundly mistrustful of aesthetic representations of the Holocaust; the potential for vulgarization, he argues, is inescapable. He is also mistrustful of historical explanations and lists of causes and effects that presume to comprehend the Holocaust. The mandate of the original commission appointed by President Carter did not specify a museum as the necessary vehicle for memorialization. Although Wiesel allowed himself to be pulled in the direction of a museum, his own intuitions favored a memorial, an architecturally constructed space with sparing, evocative use of textual passages and photographic images. In such a space a visitor would commune with the sacred memory of the horror, which would remain wrapped in its indecipherable mystery. In contrast, the museum idea, which was born in the European Enlightenment and perfected in the great museums of America, rested upon the fundamental enterprise of showing things and telling their story. Representation and pedagogy are at the essence of the endeavor. Like the imposing and ingenious exhibits of the Smithsonian Institution that would flank it on the Mall, a Holocaust museum would have to display artifacts, explain them, and integrate them into a coherent narrative. It would have to work with the expectations for clarity and instruction brought to the museum by visitors who come from all over America to visit the nation's capital and its great institutions.

It was the threshold of the visitors' sensitivities that the museum planners had to gauge in designing the exhibits. How much horror could be tolerated? There was the concern that if the museum became known principally as place where visitors were forced into a shocking exposure to atrocity that few would come and the opportunity for education would be lost. There were heated debates among the staff about how much of the horror could be withheld without compromising the story the museum was responsible for telling. A critical compromise involved the use of "privacy walls"; these were recessed video monitors that could be viewed only if a visitor approached a barrier and peered over it to see the display. These were used to present footage of Nazi medical experiments and the operations of the mobile killing squads in the East in which Jews were forced to remove their clothes and stand naked over open pits while they were machine-gunned. These scenes would not be available to children because of their physical positioning, and adults could choose not to be exposed to them.

The choice of the photomural that opens the exhibit and precedes the entire narrative of the Holocaust is a good example of the museum's internal struggles. The first candidate was a striking color photograph taken a few days after the liberation of Buchenwald that shows a disoriented group of GIs in dark uniforms standing before a truckload of skeletal white corpses piled in neat rows. The photograph had strong advocates among the staff who argued that this image of the American liberators discovering the horror of the camps was the right one with which to keynote the museum's exhibits. In the end, however, it was decided that the white flesh of the corpses with their exposed genitalia constituted too great an assault on the sensibilities of the entering visitor. The photograph was replaced with another, less shocking one in black and white that shows American soldiers standing around a pyre in which the remains of charred bodies are visible.[11]

The juxtaposition of the American soldiers and the emaciated corpses signifies one of the main objectives of the museum: to make the Holocaust relevant to the American nation. Although the United States was a bystander nation like many others, the main drama of the murder of European Jewry nevertheless took place elsewhere, and special efforts had to be made to justify the museum's symbolic and real location on the Mall in Washington alongside institutions whose Americanness was self-evident. An architectural detail illustrates the challenge and the dilemma. The building as a whole, which was designed by James Ingo Freed, at once fits into its surroundings and tell its own story. The limestone facade is somber and monumental in a way that does not jar with the other federal buildings in its vicinity; but the building's interior and the external structures that are not evident from the street are constructed out of metal and brick and exposed fixtures that evoke the industrial installations of the Nazi killing centers. A component of the museum is the Hall of Remembrance, an austere, cavernous space in which visitors are urged to meditate on what they have experienced at the conclusion of their visit. In the original design of the high, windowless external walls of the Hall of Remembrance the architect has incised two window casements that are filled in with red brick as an allusion to the ghettos of Eastern Europe. For some members of the commission, Freed's design admitted no nuance of hope; his hermetic walls sealed off contact with the adjacent monuments of American history. They wanted the structure to be opened up to those symbols of America at the same time as they wanted to protect the Mall from contamination by so stark a tragedy; for his part, Freed wanted to save the Hall of Remembrance from being transformed into "an American space" so that the intensity of the discoveries and realizations made by the visitor should not be too easily dissipated before reentering the world of official Washington. In the end, Freed agreed to change brick to limestone, but he refused to open up the windows.[12]

The desire to let in some rays of hope is intrinsic to the enterprise of the Holocaust museum. There must be some lessons that can be drawn from the tragedy. There must exist some models of righteous behavior. There must be some canons of morality that counter the reign of evil. Although the museum's narrative resists an abandonment to moral uplift, it does offer sources of consolation, and these it finds drawn from the idea of America. There is, to be sure, a forthright treatment of America's reluctance to accept refugees and the insensitivity to the fate of Europe's Jews. But the overwhelming presentation of Americans is in their role as liberators. The permanent exhibit is divided into three floors. The visitor begins with an exhibit on the rise of Nazism, then descends a floor to learn about the ghettos and concentration camps, and then descends another floor to study the aftermath of the war. There are many topics that are covered in this last venue: gentile rescuers from many countries, the war crimes trials, the immigration of survivors and their reconstructed lives in America and elsewhere. What stands out from among all these is the arrival of American army units as liberators of the camps. The concept of Americans as liberators is something of a semantic inflation. The discovery of the camps was a secondary or even accidental consequence of the American army's march eastward after the Normandy invasion; the GIs and their commanders were shocked at what they discovered not only because of its inherent monstrosity but because the concentration camps had never been part of the strategic plan and information about them had not been widely disseminated. Despite America's equivocal record in carrying out the war crimes tribunals, in admitting Nazi collaborators into the United States after the war, and in making it difficult for survivors to gain admission, the mystique of American liberation and deliverance pervades the conclusion of the museum's narrative. The museum's architecture and exhibit halls are remarkable for their consistently somber use of grays, blacks, and browns. The only exception to this stark palette is a triumphant display of gaudily colored banners representing the army units that participated in the liberation of the camps.

The museum that opened to the public in 1993 was therefore the result of many tugs and many pulls, and it remains the most powerful example of how the Holocaust is being absorbed into American historical memory. The institution that resulted from this play of opposing claims has, in any case, become an enormously popular success; it is one of the most sought-after museums in a museum-saturated city. And at a time when federal funding for arts and culture was being slashed, the museum saw its appropriations redoubled by Congress; Holocaust remembrance, at least for the time being, has held as a point of moral consensus between right and left. The museum remains a multivalent enterprise.

Some Jewish visitors object to the absence of references to cultural and spiritual resistance especially in the ghettos; others take issue with the fact that thousands of years of Jewish civilization are represented by this one instance of mass victimization. Yet for the overwhelming majority of non-Jewish visitors, the busloads of Midwestern high school students making the rounds of the Bureau of Printing and Engraving, the FBI building, and the Air and Science Museum, the Holocaust museum is now an obligatory, even normalized part of their visit to the nation's capital. What they take in there cannot easily be forgotten, but it can only be taken in to begin with because it has been made into an American story.

The Washington museum is only the largest and most ambitious in a network of Holocaust museums, memorials, and centers that have arisen since the late 1970s. Some, like the Museum of Tolerance of the Simon Wiesenthal Center in Los Angeles, were founded by Jewish organizations with a distinct point of view; others, like the Holocaust Education Center in Providence, Rhode Island, are funded agencies of the organized Jewish community; still others, like the new Museum of the Holocaust and Jewish Heritage in New York City, reflect a combination of private initiative and public municipal support. As in the case of the tangled history of the U.S. Holocaust Memorial Museum in the nation's capital, each of these institutions has its own story to tell that reflects a unique mix of local politics and communal forces with the imprint of civic leaders and prominent survivors. And like the Washington museum, each memorial has a prehistory of competing claims and negotiated compromises that has resulted in a particular configuration of Holocaust memory; each is a kind of text in which the discerning eye can observe the choices made and the models emulated.[13]

From Silence to Salience

Education is a central component of all of these institutions. Within the orbit of Jewish education specifically—in schools, youth movements, and summer camps—the Holocaust has come to be "used" extensively to sensitize young people to the events of modern Jewish history and to connect them to their heritage. This practice has occasioned debate within the community as to whether the visceral impact of the Holocaust is being inappropriately relied upon as a way of engendering Jewish identity because other measures, originating in the substance of Jewish religion and culture, have failed to do so. The most powerful weapon in the Jewish educational arsenal is the pilgrimage to the concentration camps of Middle and Eastern Europe, a trip that has been taken also by increasing numbers of adults. There is a popular and populous program called the March of the Living, which brings high school students from both America and Israel first on an intensive, emotionally laden tour of European Holocaust sites and then on a visit to Israel, so as to enact the dramatic passage from destruction to homeland.

Yet it is not within the Jewish community alone that Holocaust education takes place. Teaching about the Holocaust (together with the history of African-Americans and Native Americans) in the public schools is mandated in over seventeen states and carried out voluntarily in many more. There is a national center in Brookline, Massachusetts, called Facing History and Ourselves that produces a Holocaust curriculum for use in the schools. The "lessons" of the Holocaust presented in this public setting are obviously different from those taught in Jewish educational institutions. The goal is not to become a better Jew who identifies more closely with the Jewish people but to become a better American who understands the implications of the Holocaust for man's treatment of his fellow man. The meaning of the Holocaust is thus particularized in one setting and universalized in another.

The most significant instrument in the diffusion of Holocaust education was the appearance of the film *Schindler's List* in 1993. The film, which will be discussed in detail in chapter 3, was a watershed

From Silence to Salience

event on many scores. The Academy Awards it garnered in such profusion signaled the crossover of the Holocaust into a new prominence and acceptability—and even glamour—in the mainstream of American culture. The film was made on the strength of—and within the categories of—the filmmaker's extraordinary record as an American mythmaker. The film also capped a fateful shift, which had been in the making for some time, from a focus on the victims who had perished in the Holocaust to the victims who had survived and to the Christian rescuers who had abetted their survival. This shift was powerfully institutionalized by director Steven Spielberg himself when, building on the work of others, he created an organization to locate survivors, record their testimony on videotape, and digitalize the tapes to make them accessible as a data bank of information for research and memorialization.

Schindler's List was also unique as an educational enterprise. NBC-TV had accompanied the screening of *Holocaust* in 1978 with background materials and discussion guides. But nothing approached the waves of bundled materials, together with videotaped copies of the film itself, that were distributed free to high schools, libraries, and other educational institutions throughout the land. The study guides functioned as a powerful means for Spielberg to broadcast the film's message, or at least his conception of it. From among the many meanings of this complex work, Spielberg sought to focus attention on the universalist theme. The lesson taught by *Schindler's List,* and by extension, by the Holocaust altogether, is a lesson about man's inhumanity to man that should instruct us about hatred and intolerance in all walks of life and in relations among all groups. This, in the end, is the American teaching of the Holocaust, and it is not accidental that a Jew who is one of the most successful American film directors of all time should be the one to convey it to the American people.

2

Two Models in the Study of Holocaust Representation

For philosophers and theologians, the unprecedented enormity of the Holocaust changed everything. All of the assumptions that we carried with us from the nineteenth century into the present—assumptions about the nature of God and humanity, the progress of the human endeavor, the sanctity of art, the vocation of culture, the place of the Jews among the nations—all of these were shattered or turned inside out by Auschwitz and its crematoria. The Holocaust thus constituted a "tremendum," an event of such awful negative transcendence that it cleaved history into a before and after. That we view the present through a profoundly altered lens goes without saying, but we also cannot escape viewing the past through the medium of this terrible knowledge. All human achievement and aspiration before the event, and for Jews especially, the record of the covenantal relations between God and Israel, must be reunderstood retroactively under the sign of the Holocaust.[1]

Yet if the Holocaust is indeed a "rupture in the very fabric of being," as the philosophers have taught us, then this is a teaching that has been largely ignored for most of the half century since the war. To state this is not to be flip or anti-intellectual but to point to a fundamental truth about how cultures behave. For however persuasively we may posit the Holocaust as a paradigm-shattering tragedy,

Two Models of Holocaust Representation

it is not in the conservative nature of cultures to be easily shattered and reconfigured. It is far more typical for cultures to resist admitting the Holocaust precisely because of this subversive quality; and when the Holocaust is finally let in, and then only gradually, it enters not on its own terms, scorching earth and blazing new ground, but within the terms already set out from within the culture's own dynamic.

The case in point is the record of postwar American culture surveyed in chapter 1. In that survey I attempted to give an account of why the Holocaust moved from the margins to the center of American culture. Among the factors that encouraged this shift I counted the experience of victory at the close of the war, the new opportunities for integration opened to American Jews, the Eichmann trial, the rise of the civil rights movement, the protest against the war in Vietnam, the response of American Jewry to the Six-Day War, the reception of the stage and movie versions of Anne Frank's diary, the emergence of the survivor as a hero of culture, the broad impact of key media events on television and motion pictures, and the role of the Holocaust as a point of moral consensus between political parties and orientations. My survey aimed at synthesizing my own observations about this complex phenomenon with those of others in order to render a coherent narrative account. It is, admittedly, an interpretation that can be judged on the strength of its explanatory power. Other informed interpreters would doubtlessly give greater weight to some factors and less to others. They might, for example, amplify the role of survivors and their "second-generation" offspring in bringing attention to the Holocaust, or they might demur from my emphasis on the impact of the Eichmann trial. There might be a different valuation placed on works of high culture rather than popular culture.

Yet however the tale is told, one thing remains clear: this is an indelibly American tale. It would be unthinkable to analyze the response to the Holocaust in America without taking into consideration postwar economic conditions, the Cold War preoccupation

Two Models of Holocaust Representation

with communism and the Soviet Union, domestic protest movements, the centrality in America of television and film, the political leverage of the organized American Jewish community, U.S. policy toward Israel and the Arab world, and many other factors that are particular to the American scene. In a similar vein, it would be equally unthinkable to examine the Holocaust in Poland without considering Polish self-perceptions as victims of Nazism and the imposition of Soviet communism; or to look at the case of France without considering the mystique of the resistance and the disavowal of Vichy; or the former Soviet Union without an understanding how the Jewish identity of Jewish victims of Hitler was suppressed in the remembrance of the Great Patriotic War.

On the face of it, this would seem to be self-evident: it is simply a matter of basic responsibility in taking context into consideration in understanding the impact of the Holocaust. Yet behind this question, I would argue, lies a fundamental difference of approach as to how we should evaluate cultural responses to the Holocaust. This is a difference with far-ranging consequences for how we conceive of and constitute the enterprise of Holocaust studies generally. In the following pages, I conceptualize this difference as a tension between two models of inquiry. One I call the exceptionalist model and the other I call the constructivist model. I want to make clear at the outset that I am trafficking here in heuristic models and not in descriptions of the critical practice of any individuals, even though I shall shortly take two specific anthology projects as illustrative examples. Using binary and opposing categories is always a dangerous intellectual procedure, because it is always possible to argue that there are other, irreducible categories that are either ignored or would enrich the explanatory grid. While keeping these cautions in mind, I would argue that there is a great deal to be gained from my intentional heuristic reductionism. Given the mystified and involuted state of critical thinking about the Holocaust, it is best to begin with gross distinctions and then make room for nuanced complexity.

The exceptionalist model is rooted in a conviction of the Holocaust as a radical rupture in human history that goes well beyond notions of uniqueness. The Nazi will to murder all the Jews and the abyss of abasement inflicted upon the victims place the Holocaust in a dimension of tragedy beyond comparisons and analogies. In the black hole of this concentrationary universe, the very humanness of humanity was annihilated along with cultural rootedness. For the victims who were not killed, life in the aftermath was forever shattered no matter how successful its outer trappings. The truth about the Holocaust is a horror that few can abide without some palliative. True artistic responses to the catastrophe are rare, and they are necessarily bleak and unadorned and resist the temptation to uplift or to offer false comfort in its many forms. Hewn out of the same void, these works of art, no matter their different origins or languages of composition, make up a canon of Holocaust literature with a shared poetics. When it comes to cultural refractions of the Holocaust, however, the norm is, sadly, vulgarization, especially in works of popular culture. Most disturbing and most prevalent, moreover, is the way the Holocaust is traduced by being appropriated to serve purposes—national interests, universalist ethics, personal identity—that are not only unrelated to the Holocaust but often antithetical to its memory.

The constructivist model stresses the cultural lens through which the Holocaust is perceived.[2] The Holocaust may in fact be an unprecedented event in human history, yet it is in the nature of individuals and institutions to perceive even unprecedented events through categories that already exist. Even in accounts of the concentration camps, the place where identity was almost blotted out, such pre-existing factors as educational background, religious outlook, and native language fundamentally shape the ways the experience is represented. This is true as well for the surviving victims, whose lives, despite the unspeakable sufferings and losses during the war, display remarkable continuities alongside the inevitable changes. If the cultural lens is operative even for the victims, how much more so is it for bystanders, those who observed the grim transaction between

Two Models of Holocaust Representation

perpetrators and victims but were not directly party to it. Cultures, like individuals, can of necessity comprehend historical events only from within the set of their own issues and interests; the very willingness to engage an external event must be motivated by an internal exigency. The typical response is first denial and resistance; when the Holocaust is eventually "admitted," it is inevitably in the form of an appropriation that at once connects to the Holocaust and uses it for ulterior motives. The result might be serious or vulgar, but it will always be an appropriation. In the study of artistic responses to the Holocaust, therefore, language is key, because it is within the set of values and discursive practices embedded in a particular language and its literary traditions—be it Yiddish, Hebrew, French, Italian, Polish, German, or English—that the artist struggles to represent the Holocaust and to communicate with an audience that shares his or her language. Although the artist may seek to subvert those values and practices under the force of the Holocaust experience, the subversion can take place and make sense only within the cultural medium in which it is enacted. Similarly, acts of Holocaust memorialization, whether in the form of museums, monuments, or days of remembrance, will always reflect as much about the community that is doing the remembering as the event being remembered.

These two models rest upon very different theoretical assumptions. For the constructivist model, the point of departure is the assumption that beyond their factual core, historical events, even the Holocaust, possess no inscribed meanings; meaning is constructed by communities of interpretation—differently by different communities—out of their own motives and needs. The exceptionalist model, in contrast, discovers in the Holocaust a dark truth that inheres in the event. To be sure, there may be different versions of this truth among serious students of the event who similarly decline to be seduced by false comfort. But this vision is nevertheless not open to being coopted and constructed for other needs and purposes. Although the vision may be refracted through the lens of different cultures, it is possible to hold these amalgams up to the light of criticism and discern the elements that are true to the Holocaust experience and those that have been wrapped around it for different purposes.

Now, as explanatory frameworks, each of these models has its own strengths, and an interplay between the two is evident in the best work by students of Holocaust literature. This balanced dialectic, however, is a recent development. In the first decades of serious study of Holocaust materials the exceptionalist model held sway. After the earlier decades of silence, there was a perceptible need to arouse readers to the enormity of the horror, to make claims for the moral and aesthetic authority of these works, and to stake out their difference from the other literature of war and calamity in our century. In addition, the exceptionalist model had and continues to have great prophetic appeal. It exhorts us to remain loyal to an authentic but difficult truth and to eschew relativism, false consciousness, and opportunism when they threaten to compromise that truth. This moral high ground is shared by elite academic critics with an enduring popular sentiment that bristles at the idea that the murder of European Jewry can be taken on anything other than its own horrific terms.

The dominance of the exceptionalist model has had far-ranging effects on our understanding of Holocaust culture. It is my purpose in this chapter to lay out and explore the consequences of this disparity and to argue for the utility of the constructivist model as a counterbalance. I first elaborate on the two models by contrasting the anthologies of Holocaust literature compiled by Lawrence Langer and David Roskies. I then proceed to examine the consequences of the application of these two models in five different arenas of Holocaust studies: (1) the role of cultural difference in the literature of the concentration camps; (2) the privileging of the study of the camps over the ghettos; (3) the interplay between continuity and discontinuity in survivor narratives; (4) the shaping of the canon of Holocaust literature and its consequences for curricula, graduate training, and museum exhibitions; and (5) the status of the

Two Models of Holocaust Representation

responses to the Holocaust in American culture, especially the representation of the Holocaust in the popular media.

It needs to be mentioned before we begin that the very legitimacy of Holocaust literature did not have an easy time establishing itself. Already by the 1960s there was a significant body of writing relating to the Holocaust, although much of the work had not been translated into English. Yet the same factors that joined together to keep the Holocaust out of the mainstream of American life at that time kept works of literature on the subject on the margins of academic and intellectual discourse. Individual works were read—often read obsessively—by individual readers; and some of those works attained the status of underground classics. But there was resistance to recognizing the phenomenon as a whole, and this came from two sources. The first was an attitude that viewed the very idea of art "based" on the Holocaust with radical suspicion. Theodor Adorno's famous statement that to write poetry after Auschwitz is barbaric—despite that fact that Adorno did not mean it in the categorical way it was often taken—represented a widespread contemporary sentiment. There is no art, no matter how severe, that does not create some beauty or pleasure, if only at the level of form rather than content; and beauty and pleasure, it was averred, should not be derived from atrocity. All art, moreover, involves some artifice and rearranging of the facts in the imaginative reworking of reality. Precisely because the horror of the Holocaust was unprecedented, the proper response, it was felt, was to document that horror rather than transfigure it in any way. The second reservation related not to artistic responses to the Holocaust, which were steadily multiplying despite these suspicions, but to their critical study. The dryly analytical methods used in the academy for studying literature should not be applied to works of art that emanate from the dark mystery of the Holocaust. These works are messages from the void that are supposed to create an aura and make an impact on the reader's emotion. To submit them to the apparatus of literary criticism is to trespass

Two Models of Holocaust Representation

upon an unspoken cordon of respect for the dead in the horror of their dying.

Although this resistance continues among some general readers, in the academy the idea of the critical study of Holocaust literature has largely been accepted. The sheer number of serious works of fiction in many languages about the Holocaust that have continued to be produced makes it difficult to avoid it as a body of work. Poetry has always had an easier time of it because it was viewed, rightly or wrongly, as being expressive rather than representational, and because the verse of such poets as Paul Celan, Dan Pagis, and Nelly Sachs has manifestly needed glossing and interpretation in order to be understood. The case for taking fiction seriously has been made by critics such as Alvin Rosenfeld, Lawrence Langer, Sidra DeKoven Ezrahi, David Roskies, James Young, and Sara Horowitz, whose strong analytic writing has demonstrated that literary critical acumen need not operate at the expense of outrage and empathy.[3] In the context of Holocaust literature, they have explored strategies of fiction—including humor, estrangement, and the grotesque—and even the "lying" component at the heart of fiction—the license to select, rearrange, and even invent; they have demonstrated how these techniques can be exploited not to take flight or avoid but to sharpen the horror in ways impossible through means that are ostensibly more loyal to the plain historical record. This project of demonstration— largely successful, I believe—was aimed at two audiences at once. One was a general audience that had to be persuaded that imaginative literature and its critical study would not traduce the aura of sacred memory; the other was an academic culture of English and comparative literature departments that had to be persuaded to "admit" works of Holocaust literature into the canon of serious literature meriting critical study.

Although the students of Holocaust literature may be united in their conviction of its importance, they are deeply divided as to what it is and how it should be studied. Which are the most important authors and the most significant texts, and in which contexts are they to be read? What, in short, is the canon of Holocaust literature? Canons, we know, are not naive formations, simply the preference of good taste over bad. Even without assuming a militantly ideological stance that views canons as a means of institutionalizing hegemony, we can say, at the very least, that different canons represent different conceptions of what are strong works of art and in which qualities that strength resides. In the case of Holocaust literature, there are two major competing conceptions of the canon. Underlying one of them, I will argue, is the exceptionalist model, and underlying the other is the constructivist model. What is at stake in how they draw the map of Holocaust literature differently is profound. It is not a matter of academic nuance as much as a quarrel over the question of what of the Holocaust most needs to be remembered.

The contrastive examples I wish to adduce are two anthologies: Lawrence L. Langer's *Art from the Ashes* and David G. Roskies's *The Literature of Destruction*.[4] Both works are large and ambitious, each containing over 650 crowded pages; and both are written by key figures whose considerable previous scholarly writing gives particular authority to their anthological efforts. These volumes, important in themselves, will provide us with two concrete instances for unfolding the assumptions and ramifications of our two models for the study of Holocaust literature. Looking at the Roskies volume first will make the differences between the two most quickly apparent.

To begin with, by the rubric "the literature of destruction" Roskies means something far more extensive than the Holocaust. He begins with responses to the destruction of the first Jerusalem temple in 587 B.C.E. in the biblical books of Lamentations and Psalms and in the classical prophets; he proceeds to the responses to the destruction of the second temple in 70 C.E. in the midrashic writings of the rabbis. He then goes on to Hebrew chronicles, liturgical poems, and consolation literature composed in response to a series of catastrophic persecutions in the Middle Ages. Next is a grouping of modern, secular literary responses to the pogroms in Russia in 1881 and 1903. The World War I period, including the Russian Revolu-

Two Models of Holocaust Representation

tion and civil war, saw the virtual destruction of traditional Jewish society in Eastern Europe; these events are the subject of a selected grouping of short stories and poems in Yiddish, Hebrew, and Russian. The remainder of the anthology, except for a short coda on Israel's War of Independence, deals with the Holocaust, emphasizing literature written in the Warsaw and Vilna ghettos rather than in or about the concentration camps. In addition to literary-historical introductions to each of the volume's twenty chapters (there are one hundred entries), each text is accompanied by notes that supply sources, explain literary allusions, and reference historical events. Rather than appearing at the bottom of the page or at the end of chapters or the volume as a whole, the notes are placed up and down the page in the margin alongside the reference that needs to be explained.

For Roskies, it need hardly be pointed out, the Holocaust literature does not stand alone but must be seen in relationship to a long record of responses to catastrophe in Jewish literature. The context, then, could not be more unambiguous. But the relationship between the murder of European Jewry and these earlier destructions is not so evident. Is the Holocaust and its responses only the latest in a series of destructions? Or is the Holocaust the great destruction that overshadows the others? What, in fact, is the shape of the Jewish "literature of destruction"? The answer lies in the way the volume is organized; the anthology reveals its intentions through the disposition of materials from different historical periods. This is the distribution by pages:

First and second temples	57
Middle Ages	43
Pogroms in Russia, 1881–1905	87
World War I and aftermath	177
Holocaust	223

This arrangement makes Roskies's modernity unmistakable. In Jewish religious culture, especially as embodied in the liturgies for

Two Models of Holocaust Representation

the summer fast day on the ninth of Av, the destruction of the Jerusalem temples is the preeminent and primal catastrophe, while all later depredations, no matter how destructive, remain echoes of the ancient calamities. Roskies has turned this tradition on its head and made ancient and medieval history into a kind of background that leads up through modern times to the Holocaust. So, in Roskies's construct of a Jewish literature of destruction two things are true: The Holocaust is indeed preeminent rather than being another in a series of catastrophes. Yet at the same time, the responses to the Holocaust can be understood only by reference to responses to these earlier events. The relevance of this contextual background, moreover, increases the closer in time to the Holocaust. It is a striking feature of the anthology that the material on the pogroms in Russia at the turn of the century and during World War I together make up a larger unit (87 + 177 = 264 pages) than the section on the Holocaust itself (223 pages).

Implicit in this inverted structure is the paradoxical assumption that the tradition and the subversion of the tradition are inextricably bound up with one another. It is in the nature of collective memory, Roskies argues, that we meet the present catastrophe armed with the symbols, archetypes, and rubrics supplied by the previous catastrophe, which we then transfigure, invert, or betray because of their inadequacy in the face of the new reality. We can bring to this encounter nothing other than the cultural materials we have been given, though they be unequal to the task; and our encounter can be understood only in terms of how we reshape, deform, or jettison those materials. This is a fierce dialectic that needs to be camouflaged in a religious tradition that privileges revelation and antiquity. So, for example, when the rabbis of the midrash faced the destruction of the second temple, they had to do so through the biblical Book of Lamentations, which was written in response to the first destruction. Lamentations was authoritative because it was a canonical text, yet it is so severe in its depiction of God's unmollified rage that the rabbis had nearly to turn it inside out with their hermeneutical techniques in order to make it yield a serviceable message of consolation.

In the modern age after faith the dialectic is more patent. The responses to the successive waves of anti-Jewish violence early in the century were written by Hebrew and Yiddish writers for readers who, like themselves, had turned from traditional faith to nationalism and socialism and the other faiths of modernity. Their rejection of the martyrology and covenantal theology they inherited from the religious tradition was not veiled by the need to vindicate received forms. Yet again, their subversions can be fully understood only in terms of what they were subverting. In some cases they secularized religious categories and appropriated their authority; in other cases they parodied those traditions; in still others they imitated the tradition by focusing on the murderousness of the gentiles. These are enormous changes, but they were so entangled with the traditions that are in the course of being found inadequate that they can be decoded only with a profound awareness of the dialectical nature of the transaction.

This explains why Roskies gives as much space in his anthology to the decades that preceded the Holocaust as to the Holocaust itself. It is in this earlier period that the modern Jewish cultural formations were created that provided the categories through which the victims of the Holocaust strove to grasp their fate. There was Bundism, communism, socialism, Zionism, European humanism, and radical acculturation, together with modernized forms of Hasidism and Lithuanian Orthodoxy, and each with multiple and overlapping variations and inflections. The issue here is not so much ideological doctrine as the way in which these outlooks determined a cultural frame of reference through which individuals and communities understood the world around them. To take examples solely from the Ringelblum archive of the Warsaw Ghetto, there is one writer who experiences his hunger by contrast to an Arthur Schnitzler novel he is reading in German; another whose point of reference for the horrific sight of the ghetto being put to torch by the Germans is

Two Models of Holocaust Representation

the epic scenes of modern cinema; another who inveighs against the ghetto leadership in language borrowed from the prophetic verse of Chaim Nachman Bialik, the great poet of the Hebrew revival; and still another who, though secular, invokes the image of the Yizkor, the communal prayer for the dead, as an ultimate gesture.[5]

In all of these cases, what is both moving and innovative is the tension between the received cultural frame, on the one hand, and the awful reality that was unfolding in unprecedented ways and what the writer does with this tension, on the other. Even in the death camps, where men and women were reduced to the most primitive level of existence, prisoners viewed their situation through the lens of their upbringing and their commitments. If in the camps, then all the more so in the ghettos. This is the reason why Roskies devotes more space to the latter rather than the former. For it was in the ghettos, unlike the camps, that Jews were forced to live without significant internal interference as to the form their cultural life took. It is this highly circumscribed zone of cultural desperation that Roskies finds more interesting and revealing than the radically individuated and nearly sub-biological regime of the camps.

The role of language and cultural reference are therefore critical for Roskies. For him, language is destiny—and memory. The choice to write in Yiddish or Hebrew as opposed to Polish, German, or Russian determines not only the audience but also the entire repertoire of sources, allusions, and speech habits that are available to the writer to convey the message. So deeply are the cultural practices of earlier eras embedded in the conservative medium of language that leaving them behind is not really possible. The writer who strives to write in a radically dissociated and displaced style that owes nothing to the past and reflects the denuded world of the camps is inescapably stuck with the residual integuments that words bring with them. He or she must work against them, around them, or through them; there is no choice. Translation can do only so much. Even the best literary translators, endeavoring to create vivid English texts rather than literal equivalents, will necessarily have to make immense renunciations. It therefore falls to editors, compilers, and anthologists to provide annotation that will fill in some of the gaps. Short of saturating a text with commentary, no editor can hope to gloss the nuances and associations words bring them. It is possible, however, to note selectively crucial allusions to texts, cultural practices, and historical events. Because Roskies believes that writers inevitably undertake their encounter with the Holocaust with their responses to previous catastrophes in hand, the editor cannot do otherwise.

Lawrence Langer does in fact do otherwise, and for reasons that are consistent with a very different conception of Holocaust literature. The greatest difference between Langer's *Art from the Ashes* and Roskies's *The Literature of Destruction* is the very location of the object to be anthologized. For Roskies, Holocaust literature is situated toward the end of a long—and mostly Hebraic—tradition of responses to catastrophe in Jewish literature; although this belated literature is largely not continuous with the tradition, it remains incomprehensible without it. For Langer, Holocaust literature is a body of work unto itself; what came before is far from irrelevant, but the antecedents pale into insignificance compared with what works of Holocaust art hold in common. The black hole, the *anus mundi*, to which all acts of Holocaust writing refer, is the great, determining fact and not the cultural provenance of the writing, which, in any case, is swept away by enormity of the event. Because the *univers concentrationaire* was a world unto itself with its own language and its own laws, which resembled nothing else that humanity has devised on earth, it then follows that the literature that represents this world should form its own category with its own poetics.

Langer accordingly organizes his anthology not historically but rather by genre. There are six genres. In addition to fiction, poetry, and drama, Langer includes sections on documentary writing, journals and diaries, and the painters of Terezin. Langer opens *Art from the Ashes* with the section on documentary writing, which he calls simply "The Way It Was." It includes nonfiction writing (Charlotte Delbo, Christopher Browning, Primo Levi, Jean Amery, Elie Wiesel,

Two Models of Holocaust Representation

and others) dealing with the work of the mobile killing squads and life and death in the death camps. The second section is devoted to selections from the diaries of Abraham Lewin, Jozef Zelkowicz, and Avraham Tory, which describe deportations and *aktions* in the ghettos of Warsaw, Lodz, and Kovno, respectively. Langer intends these testimonies to form a kind of a standard, "a ballast for the chorus of fictional, dramatic, and poetic voices that succeeds it."[6] The imaginative literature that follows in the volume has been selected not only because of its "artistic quality" and "intellectual rigor" but also because it remains loyal to this essential vision of atrocity. For Langer, the truth of the Holocaust is about the defeat of hope and the victory of meaningless death. Langer is unrelenting in his contempt for sentimentality and such "safe props" as love triumphing over hate or the romantic rebellion against evil or the cult of Anne Frank. But he is also opposed to writing that casts Holocaust experience within such rubrics as "character and moral growth" and "suffering and spiritual identity."[7] Even a concept like "the tragic nature of experience" is suspect because it implies moral agency; similarly, the common notion of the concentration camps as hell is mistaken because the Christian conception of hell implied a moral universe in which punishments matched misdeeds. Wresting meaning from suffering, Langer admits, is a universal need. Yet in the instance of the Holocaust, it is a false comfort and a temptation to be resisted; Langer assesses the achievement of works of Holocaust literature according to the strength of their refusal to derive meaning. The ways in which Jews have met their deaths under conditions of persecution in the past and the narratives they have constructed to make sense out of these calamities have no relevance. "Myth and tradition," Langer states tersely, "are of little use in consoling them [the victims] or us."[8]

Langer's exceptionalist vision also determines the nature of his editorial treatment of the texts he anthologizes. He introduces each author and locates his or her work within the world of the Holocaust, but the texts themselves remain barren of annotation. Absent are the kind of references that stud the pages of Roskies's

Two Models of Holocaust Representation

anthology: verses, sources, and traditional allusions as well as references to the specifics of contemporary events. This is true in part because of Langer's criteria of inclusion. To begin with, he selects *out* all writing that makes extensive use of "myth and tradition," even if these are invoked only to be subverted or parodied. Still, the texts he does bring into the canon display many points that would have elicited annotation had they been dealt with by a different editorial hand. How then are we to understand his restraint? There can be no question of dereliction on Langer's part; there is no custodian of Holocaust texts more respectful and responsible than he. The implication, I think, is that these references—which, in the end, are the cultural differentiae of their authors—are not essential, certainly not essential to the general reader, to grasping the core experience of the text. That experience is about the annihilation of humanity and the obliteration of received cultural constructions, and in the margins of this drama of extremity glosses on those constructions make little contribution.

Langer's position asserts itself most radically when it comes to the question of translation. This issue is not the generally high quality of the translations Langer has selected for his anthology but the fact of translation itself. All but one or two of the texts in the volume have been translated into English; the languages of the originals span the languages of Hitler's victims: German, Czech, Yiddish, Hebrew, French, Italian, Hungarian, and so on. Yet try as one might, it is only by resourceful detective work that the reader can discover the language in which a given text was originally written. Biographical notes are not a sure enough base upon which to make accurate inferences. Is it so clear that a Jew growing up in Hungary will write in Hungarian and not German? Or that a Jew growing up in Transylvania will take on French as a literary language? Or that a Jew from Czernowitz will write in Hebrew? Even with persistence it is still impossible without prior knowledge to discover the original language of at a least a half dozen of the selections. The names of the translators—but not the languages translated from—are listed only in the small print of

Two Models of Holocaust Representation

the copyright acknowledgments in the front matter of the volume and not in the body of the book. Again, this is not negligence but a kind of principled indifference. If the Holocaust constitutes a separate realm—or planet or universe, whatever the metaphor may be—then it has its own language, a language that is displaced and unnatural but at the same time unmistakable. Although there is a price to be paid for reading all of these documents in English, it is a price that is paid equally across the board, and it is far from being the renunciation it would have been in an earlier era when the echoes and nuances of cultural traditions counted for more.

If one is inclined to be sympathetic when it comes to prose, it is harder to do so in the case of poetry's intricate verbal artistry. Yet Langer is unremitting even here. He includes selections from six poets: Abraham Sutzkever and Jacob Glatstein in Yiddish, Paul Celan and Nelly Sachs in German, Dan Pagis in Hebrew, and Miklos Radnoti in Hungarian. The linguistic situation of each of these poets—the languages they grew up with in relation to the language they chose to write in as opposed to the languages of the milieu in which they wrote—is, to say the least, complicated. For Langer, however, their orientation toward a single, transformative event is the key.

> They are linked by the premise of a people's extermination, and by the need to enter into what Paul Celan called a "desperate conversation" with their audience—a conversation that evidently has already occurred within their own imaginations. *This bond reduces, if it does not eliminate, the cultural differences separating poets writing in Hebrew, Yiddish, German, and Hungarian.*[9] (emphasis added)

Langer's statement about poetry presents an image of poets in different languages being "linked" together in a common "bond" by the destruction of European Jewry, their separateness transcended by a universal experience. Yet at the same time this is a solidarity that is purchased at the expense of the debasement of the linguistic medium that creates the connection. Words may be all that remain after

Two Models of Holocaust Representation

Auschwitz, but their aura, their power, and their difference have been vastly leveled and reduced.

I have presented these two anthological projects to illustrate in a pragmatic way the differences between the exceptionalist and constructivist models in the study of Holocaust culture. Of the two, Langer's exceptionalist point of departure is the more immediately evident. The constructivist foundation of Roskies's work needs more elaboration. It is important to point out, to begin with, that Roskies's *The Literature of Destruction* realizes only one line of sight among many other possibilities. He has reconstructed a cultural continuum and context from within which Jews from a particular geographical sphere with certain kinds of literacy and outlooks would experience the Holocaust. These tend to be—I generalize, but not overmuch—Jews from Eastern Europe who are native Yiddish speakers (as well as being Hebraically literate), intellectuals and citizens of modernity who identify with Jewish nationalism in its Bundist or Zionists forms. Roskies attempts to reconstruct the relevant Jewish past and present as they would have seen it on the eve of the war and in the midst of the ghettos. In the far distance are the ancient destructions and the archetypal figures and terms of reference they established; more vivid and closer at hand are the pogroms and persecutions of modern memory, which in turn invoke both the martyrologies of the Middle Ages and the ideologies of recent times. This is the cultural lens through which this set of victims experienced their fate—and remembered it as well, for those who survived—and this is also the set of cultural materials out of which and against which they fashioned a response to that fate.

Being specific about the identity of the subjects of Roskies's anthology makes it easier to imagine the many alternative constructions that are possible. The métier of Roskies's subjects is Yiddish; if one shifts the focus to Hebrew, then a related but very different construction looms large. The cultural lens then becomes the Zionist interpretation of history with its harsh judgment of the exile-ridden passivity of East European Jews. The poetic descriptions of the

Two Models of Holocaust Representation

Kishenev pogrom in 1903 by the national poet of the Hebrew revival Chaim Nachman Bialik will provide the standard stock of images. Survivors will undertake their work of remembrance against the grain of stigma and avoidance in the new, forward-looking society of Israel.[10] An entirely different perspective comes into view if the subject is changed to traditional religious Jews, whether Hasidic or non-Hasidic. Their understanding of the Holocaust, viewed retrospectively or from within the depths of the event itself, configures the past differently, privileging biblical promises and consolations and refurbishing medieval mystical teachings concerning God's concealment as well as His empathy. Their determination to replicate and even surpass the religious institutions that existed before the destruction locates this community within a different continuum. And so the examples of hypothetical anthologies could be multiplied: the anthology of the acculturated German Jews with their traditions of Enlightenment and belief in civil society and devotion to the German language; the anthology of Soviet Jews, who saw the conflict as part of the great patriotic war against fascism and imagined the past as a time that was divided by the period before the Revolution and after; the anthology of Viennese Jews and Jews from other lands formerly under the Hapsburg Empire. Each of these hypothetical anthologies, and others that could be easily added to them, would constitute a different kind of lens that refracts the Holocaust differently and recalls the Jewish past differently because of the different nature of the Jewish community's relationship to modernity and to the particular gentile society that surrounds it. This would hold true for America as well. Like Israel, America is a bystander community with a survivor minority. How America, whether one speaks of the Jewish community (and its subcommunities) or the nation as a whole, constructs the Holocaust will then necessarily be deeply colored by the issues, long antedating the Holocaust as well as succeeding it, that animate American society.

Langer's position, if I can take leave to imagine what it might be, would regard these various anthologies as interesting and worthwhile

Two Models of Holocaust Representation

but, in the end, beside the point—if the point is the Holocaust itself. Each anthology is at bottom a plotting of the collective memory of a discrete interpretive community; it demonstrates how a group, with its proprietary issues and interests, appropriates the Holocaust and reconfigures the past, both the pre-Holocaust past and the more recent post-Holocaust past, to make sense of the present. It is the act of appropriation which, in addition to being offensive to Langer on moral grounds, points in a direction away from the core experience of the Holocaust. That experience is about "the way it was" in the eye of the storm as experienced by individuals, who, stripped of their family and community, faced their fate without the consolations of "myth and traditions." The temporal extensions backward and forward, the retrojection of the Holocaust into the past and the solvent action of present memory, are not unimportant; to the contrary, they can be revealing as cultural data, but they belong to something other than the representation of the Holocaust as such.

There is an illuminating sense in which Langer's own project in *Art from the Ashes* can also be thought of as a kind of special-interest anthology of a culturally specific community. That community, however, is nothing less than the polity of the West and its tradition of humanism. As reflected in Langer's anthology and his other writings, especially the essays in *Versions of Survival,* the Holocaust becomes the event that refutes and shatters the idea of man as it has been established in the liberal thought of the West.[11] The belief in reason that was the legacy of the Enlightenment and the belief in the rapport of the human spirit with the world that was the legacy of Romanticism—all this was exploded by the fact of the crematoria. This is not a cultural formation that can be devolved into ethnic or religious claims; for it is precisely for the sake of this shared humanistic outlook that Jews and Protestants and Catholics from many lands and languages placed their particularist origins in the background and merged into a common aspiration. Langer's anthology is about the annihilation of the assumptions underlying this project, and it is in this sense that the anthology can be thought of as the record of a particular group, a group that included all the forward-looking men and women of modern Europe—and us, their descendents.[12]

The purpose of discussing Roskies's and Langer's anthologies has been to elaborate the implications of the constructivist and exceptionalist models for the study of Holocaust culture. We now proceed to examine the practical consequences of privileging one or the other of the models. If we have been dealing until this point with the refinement of analytic constructs, we now look to the exigent tasks of applied understanding in the five areas mentioned above: (1) the literature of the camps, (2) the claims of ghetto culture, (3) the construction of survivor narratives, (4) the conception of Holocaust studies, and (5) the reception of the Holocaust in America.

The account of death and survival in the concentration camps, to begin with, is what we know to lie at the center of Holocaust literature. It is a story about the systematic annihilation of the individual's humanity before the final act of extermination. The process began with wrenching families apart and continued with the shaving of the head, crushing labor, progressive starvation, random terror, and death. Fundamental to the Nazi design of the camp regime was the dismantling of the inmate's civilized and socialized self and his or her reduction to a cowed, animal-like state of isolated self-interest. The balance of starvation, exhaustion, and fear was calibrated to hold human existence, for an interval, just above the threshold of death and just below the threshold of memory and thought. It is here, in the nethermost darkness of a horror never before devised, that Langer and others locate the normative Holocaust experience. It is an experience in which human beings are stripped of all the integuments of identity, culture, solidarity, and belief that clothe their nakedness.

This is a presumption, I would submit, that is at odds with a fundamental aspect of the greatest writing on the camps. Tadeusz Borowski's *This Way for the Gas, Ladies and Gentlemen,* Primo Levi's *Survival in Auschwitz,* and Elie Wiesel's *Night* stand, by most all

Two Models of Holocaust Representation

accounts, at the center of the Holocaust canon and can hardly be said to shrink from the representation of atrocity. Yet for each of these writers it is cultural identity that provides the essential lens through which they focus their vision and by which we can best gain access to their work. Borowski was a humanistically educated non-Jewish Pole, Levi was a chemist from an acculturated Italian Jewish family, and Wiesel was a Talmud student from a traditionally religious family in Transylvania. Rather than simply being points of departure that are swept into the dark hole of the Holocaust, these identities—though they be assaulted, rent, and transfigured—remain fundamental ways of seeing the world and organizing experience. These narratives are inverted bildungsromans that recount the story of how the hero *unlearns* what culture has taught and learns the ways of death and survival on the new, concentrationary "planet." Yet the process of reeducation is never fully completed, for the retrospective narrator, more dead than living, has survived to write now, in the immediate aftermath of the war, about the young person he or she was then. It is through this residuum of identity that the experience is most tellingly retracted.

Take the case of Borowski, the author of some of the most searing writing about the camps. Borowski was born in the Soviet Ukraine in 1922 to parents who were both transported to Siberian labor camps when he was a child. They were released in a prisoner exchange, and the family settled in Warsaw, where Tadeusz was sent to a boarding school run by Franciscan monks. After the German occupation, Borowski attended underground university seminars and published a book of poems. Both he and his fiancée were arrested and sent to Auschwitz in the spring of 1942. Spared the gas chambers as an "Aryan," Borowski lived the life of a slave laborer whose "privileges" allowed him a degree more mobility and sustenance than Jewish inmates. The fact that Borowski's situation was located adjacent to the fate of the Jews but not within it provides his fiction with a powerful opportunity for observation. The way he exploits this distance is made all the more credible by his refusal to spare scrutiny of himself and the prerogatives enjoyed by non-Jewish prisoners. One of these was the possibility of occasional communication with his fiancée, who was an inmate in the women's camp at Auschwitz. To illustrate the issue of cultural identity, I have chosen a passage from "Auschwitz, Our Home (A Letter)" in *This Way for the Gas, Ladies and Gentlemen,* which describes camp life in the form of a letter to his fiancée.

> Do you really think that, without the hope that such a world is possible, that the rights of man will be restored again, we could stand the concentration camps even for one day? It is that very hope that makes people go without a murmur to the gas chambers, keeps them from risking a revolt, paralyses them into numb inactivity. It is the hope that breaks down family ties, makes mothers renounce their children, or wives sell their bodies for bread, or husbands kill. It is hope that compels man to hold on to one more day of life, because that day may be the day of liberation. Ah, and not even the hope for a different world, but simply for life, and life of peace and rest. Never before in the history of mankind has hope been stronger than man, but never also has it done so much harm as it has in this war, in this concentration camp. We were never taught how to give up hope, and this is why today we perish in the gas chambers.[13]

Borowski's narrator/correspondent addresses an issue that has disturbed many observers of victims' behavior in the camps. How is it, given the virtual inevitability of death as well as the tiny number of captors relative to prisoners, that there was so little resistance and rebellion? The answer, it turns out, lies not where we would be most likely to look for it: in man's essential animality and his reduction to monstrous self-interest under conditions of absolute extremity. Rather it lies in what is ordinarily counted as an admirable human impulse: the ineradicability of hope. Whether it is a primitive hope that surviving another day may bring deliverance tomorrow or an idealistic hope that a better world will be built on the ruins of the concentration camps, the effect is the same kind of denial of reality, the reality of the Nazis' programmatic intention to murder all Jews after having exacted from them the last measure of labor. Had the victims been able to admit this truth, they might have realized that they had nothing to lose in resisting, or at least in preserving the "family ties" that would otherwise be betrayed. It was hope, then, that paradoxically abetted the implementation of the extermination program. Borowski's speaker, it should be noted, offers this analysis not as a judgment censuring the victims for collusion in their fate. He is a victim, and the lover he is writing to is a victim as well; he writes as part of a communal "we" in an effort at collective self-understanding.

Now, if we read this passage with the common-sense understanding of the word *hope* in mind, it is persuasive enough on its own terms. But it becomes immensely more powerful if we understand hope in relation to Borowski's background and education. For when the speaker says at the end that we "were never taught to give up hope," he is stressing a concept of hope that derives not from instinctual biological survival but from a set of values that a culture consciously transmits to its young. For a young Pole whose parents were imprisoned by Stalin, who was educated by monks and who then studied literature in the university (or its equivalent under the occupation), *hope* is one of the most ideologically fraught terms in the modern lexicon. In the Christian tradition, it signals the hope for salvation, which will be the lot of the faithful if they believe perfectly enough despite the wickedness of the world. In Marxism, hope signals the conviction that the contradictions of capitalism will inexorably lead to its collapse and to the ascent of a just social order, and that, in the name of the unfolding of this certain hope, all means are sanctioned. In the liberal tradition of the Enlightenment and the university, hope signals the belief that the realization of man's perfectibility can be nurtured by the right kind of sentiments and social institutions. Borowski is the heir to all of these traditions, which are knotted together under the tangled signifier *hope;* so when he makes this term the prime agent of the victims' submission to their victimizers, he is making a rejection whose enormity resonates mightily. We can strive to understand this thing called hope, which must be unlearned, only if we succeed in understanding, in all its overdetermined cultural specificity, what was once so diligently acquired.

Not all that is learned is unlearned. Primo Levi takes the habit of scientific observation with him into Auschwitz and takes it with him after the liberation.[14] The awareness of the scientific voice of the narrator of *Survival in Auschwitz* was heightened by the later publication of *The Periodic Table,* which used the schemata of chemistry even more explicitly, and by Levi's postwar work as the manager of a Turin chemical factory.[15] There is simply no more persuasive example than Levi's for the argument that even the concentrationary experience is inevitably viewed through the lens of culture. Levi was raised in an acculturated Jewish family whose ancestors had come from Spain in the 1500s to settle in the Piedmont. The scientific training Levi chose for himself in the university was an expression not only of his own temperament but of the commitment of Italian Jewry as a whole to the traditions of liberal rationalism and the inheritance of the Enlightenment.

Levi was trained in his profession to observe the properties and interactions of physical substances. In Auschwitz, however, the object of Levi's observations becomes, of necessity, the moral behavior of human beings. Levi thus recapitulates in reverse the development of Enlightenment rationalism, which began expansively with the measure of humanity and society and narrowed into the methods of the exact sciences. The force of experience compels Levi to apply these observational methods to the chaos of human terror; and the enormous power of his book derives from the tension between the techniques of rationality and the eruption of radical evil embodied in the camps. Levi carries this off by making a fundamental distinction between the mind and motives of the perpetrators, whose evil can never be penetrated by reason, and the behavior of the victims, which can indeed be understood empathically as adaptations to the unspeak-

Two Models of Holocaust Representation

able conditions in which they were condemned to exist. Levi's description of the Nazis' "gigantic biological and social experiment" is governed, as Philip Roth puts it, "very precisely, by a quantitative concern for the ways in which a man can be transformed or broken down and, like a substance decomposing in a chemical reaction, lose his characteristic properties."[16] Levi's laboratory notes are not a vindication of reason but a method of coping. Through the lens of science that he acquired from his culture he is forced to see things that had never fallen within the purview of science to observe. But instead of abandoning the tools of reason, Levi clings to them in the service of memory and clarity.

In the case of Elie Wiesel, the lens of culture is bifocal. Although *Night* covers much of the same territory as other memoirs of Auschwitz, its distinctiveness lies in the way experience is focalized through the perceptions of the author's young autobiographical persona. When the Germans occupy Sighet, Eliezer is a sixteen-year-old Talmud student from a comfortable home who has been free to immerse himself in his studies and pursue a covert passion for the mystical lore of the Kabbalah. The transport to Auschwitz, the breaking apart of the family, and the torments of camp life are all presented as chapters in a process of compulsory reeducation in which the young man unlearns what he believes about God and the human race. The climactic moment of apostasy is reached in the famous scene in which Eliezer is forced to watch the hanging of a beloved little boy with the face of a "sad angel"; to the question "Where is God now?" the narrator hears a voice within himself responding, "He is hanging here on this gallows."[17]

That Wiesel frames his experience as a theological crisis at once sets him apart from writers like Borowski and Levi and makes his story understandable only in terms of who he was and where he came from. The complexity of *Night* as a phenomenon derives in part from the two different ways this crisis was refracted retrospectively. As mentioned in chapter 1, *Night* was first written in Yiddish and published within survivor circles in Argentina; Wiesel then revised and rewrote it in French with the encouragement of Christian existentialist François Mauriac, who contributed a foreword, and it was the French version that served as the basis of the English translation. There are significant differences between the Yiddish and French versions, as Naomi Seidman has pointed out, and the differences have a great deal to do with what it meant to write in Yiddish or to write in French in the 1950s.[18] To write in Yiddish meant to write for a small survivor audience that would feel at home with expressions of high pathos and share the writer's outrage at the nations of the world for standing by silently. To write in French meant to envisage a different audience and to work within the sensibility of another language. It meant to rein in the urge to accuse, to contain pathos and sentiment, and to frame the central crisis in more universal terms as the young believer's discovery of radical evil. Whether the discursive practices of one language are to be preferred over those of the other is beside the point. The point is that a constructivist approach to Wiesel's *Night* and other concentration camp literature heightens our awareness of how the "Holocaust experience," even in its most unspeakable precincts, is built up out of the materials of language and culture and focused through one among a number of possible lenses.

The very notion of the concentration camp as the prototypical site of Holocaust literature is put in question by the constructivist model. Both critical discourse and the popular imagination have long been drawn to representations of the death camps because of their ultimacy. The camp as a mechanized death factory, along with comprehensive genocide, was the Nazis' most infamous contribution to the history of persecution. In the perverted sense of a "final solution," it was also the culmination of various earlier means devised to commit mass murder. As the most extreme instance of evil, the camp—or to be more precise, one camp—became a metonymy for the Holocaust as a whole. To begin a statement with the words "After Auschwitz" is not to make a specific reference but to invoke the cat-

Two Models of Holocaust Representation

astrophe in its totality. Terrence Des Pres's seminal study *The Survivor: An Anatomy of Life in the Death Camps* (1976)[19] and much of Lawrence Langer's writing are only two examples of a large body of critical work that examines the world of the camps in writers such as Charlotte Delbo, Jean Amery, and Primo Levi and finds in it, even if in different ways and for different reasons, the essence of the Nazi assault on the Jews and on the idea of humanity. The camp has become a kind of telos, an ultimate end case, by which all proximate experience is measured.

In its critique of this notion, the constructivist model asserts that, although the world of the camps does indeed occupy the ultimate station on the continuum of horror, what it has to tell us about Jewish behavior during the Holocaust is contingent on and, in a number of crucial respects, less interesting than behavior in other venues. Whether it was starvation and sleep deprivation, the kapo system, collective reprisals for individual deviation, or any of the other components of what Des Pres calls the "excremental assault on man," the camp regime was effectively geared to obliterating consciousness and individuality and reducing human beings to submissive, half-dead automata. That some inmates were able to hold on to shreds of their humanity should not, Langer insists, distract us from the kind of fate that awaited almost all, nor should it lead to an idealization—and here Langer dissents from Des Pres—of the impulse to survive. The scope of human agency remained radically delimited and radically isolated. Despite the masses of inmates who were forced to live an insufferably thronged life, literally one atop the other, each individual faced the daily ordeal of survival in a state of deep isolation while ceaselessly pursuing his or her self-interest often at the expense of others. Instances of unselfishness, solidarity, and expressions of group identity did exist, to be sure, but the modal nature of existence in the death camps remained cut off and self-involved.

It is the literature of the ghettos that provides a crucial supplement to the literature of the camps. There were many ghettos in Eastern Europe; the situation of each was somewhat different, and

Two Models of Holocaust Representation

the kind and volume of literature and other cultural artifacts produced in them were also different. Much of what was produced did not survive and could be recovered only in accounts by survivors. The most famous instance is the Oyneg Shabes archive in the Warsaw ghetto organized by Emanuel Ringelblum and buried in the rubble of the ghetto in tin boxes and milk canisters. The archive consisted of about six thousand documents, including "eyewitness accounts and diaries; letters and postcards; sermons and songs; epic and lyric poems; novels, short stories and plays; essays, questionnaires and autobiographies; and issues of the underground Jewish press."[20] The reason there exists such a vast literature derives from a startling difference between the ghetto and the camp: within the ghetto Jews were free to conduct their own collective life. At this stage of war, the Nazis sought to concentrate the Jews and strip them of their wealth; they did not seek to control the organization and expression of internal political, social, spiritual, and cultural life, choosing instead to administer the ghettos through the intermediacy of the *judenrate*. Although terror and starvation stalked their daily lives, the Jews of the ghetto were free to organize their own forms of social welfare, put on political cabarets, hold concerts, publish uncensored newspapers, and give public sermons.

What sets the camps apart from the ghettos is not necessarily the quantum of suffering and atrocity. The camps were admittedly worse, but this is a dreadful calculus that can be figured in many ways. The difference lies in the question of control. In the camps, individuals were wrenched out of their familial and communal bonds and placed under a regime that dominated and scrutinized their every waking and sleeping moment. The discovery of the least individual expression, whether a sketch of camp life or a written document, could be grounds for punishment or death. The accounts of camp life that we have are necessarily recollections and reconstructions written at different removes after the war, and their authors, again by definition, are survivors. The ghetto documents, by contrast, are written during the actual duration of the ghetto, reflecting on and responding to events that changed with enormous rapidity. They were written overwhelmingly—it need hardly be said—by authors who did not survive the war. Most important, this literature was written from within a tightly circumscribed yet essentially free cultural space that allowed for the expression of the collective in a variety of ways. Jews could identify themselves with political parties and ideological movements, express their theological struggles, adopt the role of the social scientist and study behavior in the ghetto, compose folk and cabaret songs for public performance, write stories about life in the ghetto, keep diaries, or undertake any of a number of other forms of activity or expression, and they could do so in Yiddish, Hebrew, or Polish at different times for different purposes and audiences.

The enormous claim this literature makes on us is that it opens a window onto the experience of Jewry in real time rather than in recollected time. It is a commonplace of writing on the Holocaust to say that time has to pass, perhaps even a generation, before words can be uttered about so awful a trauma. Yet this conception is challenged by the contentious and articulate voices of the ghetto writers as they argue, document, analyze, and imagine. The contribution made by the growing profusion of survivor memoirs and videotaped testimony is invaluable, but it is necessarily subject to the selective and harmonizing operations of memory, and it is written with a global and retrospective understanding of parallel developments and final outcomes. This was precisely the kind of knowledge that actors in the drama could not have; the inhabitants of an individual ghetto could know with only very imperfect certainty what was happening at the same time to Jews elsewhere, not to mention what would be the next moves of the German administration. A ghetto like the Warsaw Ghetto was, after all, not a suspended moment but an extended duration in which the situation changed, as Ringelblum put it, "with cinematic speed." The Warsaw Ghetto was established soon after the German invasion of Poland in 1939; the Great Deportation of three hundred thousand Jews took place in the late summer of 1942; the uprising and the liquidation of the remaining

Two Models of Holocaust Representation

seventy thousand Jews took place in the spring of 1943. Stories and reportage by such writers as Simon Huberband, Leyb Goldyn, and Peretz Opoczynski describe a complex mosaic of individual and communal responses—denial, flight, lamentation, mutual aid, documentation, political organization—to a pattern of events whose unfolding was unknown.

Writing about the situation of the Warsaw Ghetto in 1942, David Roskies illuminates the multiple strands of ghetto life in a single critical moment.

> It began erev Tisha b'Av and ended on Yom Kippur: *di oyszidlung,* the Great Deportation. First the Germans demanded that 6,000 Jews be delivered to the Umschlagplatz each day, then 10,000 a day. Adam Czerniakov, head of the Judenrat, took his own life rather than sign away the lives of the children; the children—the only hope of regeneration. Dr. Janusz Korczak went to his death leading all the children of his orphanage behind him. At the end of July, the Hechalutz Youth movement organized the first combat unit. At the end of August most of the ghetto shops were closed down, thus dooming the dream that productivization would guarantee survival. The first couriers sent by the Bund and the Zionists returned from Treblinka and confirmed the rumors about the final destination of the cattle cars. At the same time, Israel Lichtenstein and a few assistants buried the first part of the Oyneg Shabes Archive in the basement of the soup kitchen for children at 68 Nowolipki Street.

Ironically, Roskies's synoptic slice of ghetto life illustrates just the kind of global, retrospective knowledge that no one of the actors could have had in its entirety at the time. Yet by simultaneously evoking the initiatives of many sectors of the ghetto at a single critical juncture, Roskies gives us a glimpse of the deeply textured nature of time as it was experienced by the ghetto's inhabitants.

One of the key features of the ghetto literature is its uncensored moral rhetoric in which names of collaborators are named and the

Two Models of Holocaust Representation

behavior of Jews toward Jews is unflinchingly described. The censorship imposed on these realities came not from the Germans, who did not care what went on inside the ghetto, but from Holocaust survivors generally in their spoken or written recollections of the war. There is a pronounced tendency in survivor testimony, the result of a number of motives, to play down the feelings of accusation and betrayal that were strongly felt at the time. These include not only the evident indictments of members of the *judenraten,* or the Jewish police, but also the polemics and controversies among political parties and groupings with rival ideologies. In this respect, the ghettos were normal Jewish communities full of contentiousness among opposing political and religious interests. The ghettos were abnormal in that they were swelled by the forced influx of surrounding communities, concentrated into a tiny space, and submitted to the pressures of a deteriorating external situation. Under these conditions, the "normative" divisiveness of communal life could only be exacerbated by an exponential factor. These are hard truths, but they have to be reckoned with in any honest understanding of the Holocaust. Ringelblum understood this and specifically instructed his staff "to write as if the war were already over, not to fear retribution from those in power because the indictment would not be read until everyone in question was either living in freedom or already dead."[21]

Nothing could stand in greater contrast to Ringelblum's charge to his staff than the urge toward discretion evident in many postwar memoirs. The anger that was once directed internally because the real aggressor was beyond reach finds an outward channel after the catastrophe. The memories of the fierce intra-Jewish conflict fade as the totality of the victims are absorbed into the aura of martyrdom and as the remembrance of past strife and perfidy seems increasingly pointless. There is no unworthiness and a great deal of naturalness in this way of remembering, and I shall have occasion later on to speak on behalf of the selective appropriation of the Holocaust past. Yet it is important to point out, as Yosef Yerushalmi has reminded us, that this kind of remembering belongs to the flow of collective memory rather than to the project of historiography. In our struggle to grasp the Holocaust, we manifestly need both, and the literature of the ghettos stands as an essential counterpart and corrective to the gathering sway of memoir.

Finally, there is the issue of cultural density. When survivors write about the concentration camps, they are usually attempting to explain a radically foreign experience to readers who are, thankfully, uninitiated in the subject; this was a world that had been emptied of all received culture and filled with a new and perverted language and moral code. However, when the inhabitants of the ghettos wrote songs, broadsides, and stories, they were—Ringelblum's exhortation aside—by and large addressing each other with words and gestures whose meaning was guaranteed by shared frames of reference. Whether it was the lexicon of Jewish socialism or Zionism, Yiddish literature, the Hebrew Bible, Hasidism, or contemporary European literature, the cultural codes in play before the war were not only not abandoned but in many cases intensified. So the secular Yiddish writer Rachel Auerbach, in contemplating the destruction of the Warsaw Ghetto and of her whole family from hiding in the Aryan side of Warsaw, is thrust back upon, despite her secularity, the image of the collective recitation of the memorial Yizkor prayer in the synagogue as the only adequate symbol for expressing her grief.[22] Or take one of the great diarists of the Warsaw Ghetto, Abraham Lewin, who switches from Yiddish to Hebrew in his diary entries after the Great Deportation.[23] When the narrator of Yehoshue Perle's brilliant satire on life in the ghetto after the Great Deportation chimes up with "I'm alright, I'm a number!" it will be intelligible to all Yiddish readers as a play on the motto ("I'm alright, I'm an orphan!") of one of Shalom-Aleichem's most famous characters, Motl, son of Peyse the Cantor.[24] Or when Chaim Kaplan, another of the preeminent diarists of the Warsaw Ghetto, writing in Hebrew, exclaims, "Oh earth! Do not hide my blood!! If there is a God to judge the land—come and take revenge!!!" no Hebrew reader can mistake the quotation from Bialik's famous poem on the Kishenev massacre of 1903.[25] Taken together, these are not the sort of recondite intertextual allusions intended for the learned; they are signals meant to be picked up by any literate person. They are simply indicators of what it means to be part of a culture.

Now, one would think that given the critical importance of this corpus it would be the object of intense study, interpretation, and reflection. For where else in the galaxy of Holocaust writing is there such a revealing body of interrelated cultural production? In light of the enormous interest in the Holocaust in America, we might have expected that the disintegrating sheets of paper in Ringelblum's milk canisters would be accorded the same care as the Dead Sea Scrolls and the fragments of the Cairo Geniza and be preserved, annotated, and translated. The fact is, however, that shockingly little is available to the English reader, and that the original documents in the original languages are very unevenly available to scholars. As far as the Warsaw Ghetto is concerned, besides the diaries of Chaim Kaplan and Abraham Lewin, there is little represented in English of Ringelblum's herculean archival effort.[26] How much is there is indicated by the simple fact that Joseph Kermish's meticulously edited Hebrew translation of the journalism published in the Warsaw Ghetto runs to six volumes.[27] Moreover, what was available in English until recently did not touch upon the belletristic works in the collection. Until Roskies published translations of texts by Yehoshue Perle, Leyb Goldin, Rachel Auerbach, and Peretz Opoczynski, stories that are by any account masterpieces of Holocaust literature could not be read in English. Again, in light of the intensive publishing activity on Holocaust matters in America, how is one to explain that it is the Poles who are slowly bringing out the Warsaw Ghetto materials in facsimile editions with annotations in Polish?

The reasons for this relative neglect are not immediately apparent. To be sure, making the ghetto materials accessible to a wider audience is not an easy job. It is not so much the task of translating from several languages as much as it is the challenge of translating the *context* in which these documents are embedded: the references to personalities, events, places, political groupings, slang, and religious practices and the textual allusions. It is not an easy job, but it is a doable job, and even a partial and selective level of annotation of the sort Roskies employs in his anthology is enough to dissolve the strangeness and allow us to penetrate the drama of ghetto life. All it takes is the individual and institutional will to undertake the project.

The problem, I suspect, lies in the embarrassment of particularity embodied by these documents. The ghetto writers describe lives that are deeply enmeshed in the very particular culture and politics of their times, and to know these lives requires acquiring some familiarity with this tangled knot of time and place and belief. When it comes to concentration camp literature, the "literacy" necessary to master the code of the *Lager,* despite the greater extremity and greater strangeness, is ironically much easier to come by. There is one primitive language and one primitive and unequivocal rule of behavior. By reading a single exquisitely observed and empathic book like Levi's *Survival in Auschwitz* one does not learn all there is to know about the concentrationary universe, but one learns enough to learn more. The life of the prisoner is a life that has been reduced to a biological core that exists before culture or beneath culture. In contrast, it is easy to perceive the embroiled particularity of life in the ghettos as not belonging to the essence of things and not demanding our best energies in its explanation and description because it remains penultimate rather than ultimate.

In his discussion of the phenomenon of "cultural resistance to genocide," Lawrence Langer adds another layer of explanation. Langer is uncomfortable with the term *resistance* because it implies "the possibility of an immediately beneficial consequence, a gesture of affirmation or defiance that might alter the condition of the poet, writer, the painter."[28] Avraham Sutzkever's composition of his Yiddish poems in the Vilna Ghetto and the production of Rabindrath Tagore's play *The Post Office,* which was mounted by

Two Models of Holocaust Representation

the orphans in the Warsaw orphanage run by Janusz Korczak before he marched with them to the transports, are admirable in many respects, Langer allows, but they must be seen in perspective. These cultural efforts, and others like them, are to be understood as attempts at self-consolation, even denial, in the face of the nameless terror they were incapable of affecting. Langer writes:

> Cultural traditions furnish a certain security and even sanctity to a life otherwise sundered from the normal props of existence. Few were able to endure on a diet of mere blank terror. The illusion that a familiar past could prepare one for an unknown future never lost its magic appeal to imaginations that had nothing else to rely on.[29]

If the most that can be claimed for culture under the sign of the Holocaust is that it offers the comfort of the familiar, then the artifacts and activities of the ghetto inhabitants cannot count for much in the face of the "blank terror" of the real thing.

The shape of survivor narratives is the third area materially affected by the divergence between the exceptionalist and constructivist models. As the survivor population has aged and as the acceptability of the Holocaust has grown, memoirs of the war years have been published in recent decades at a dizzying rate. Ambitious projects recording survivor testimony on videotape are creating a vast archive of personal narratives. We are at a stage of recording, gathering, producing, publishing, and preserving. The task of figuring out what it all means is necessarily being deferred for the present, but it is a challenge that will eventually have to be met.[30] For now, we can begin to formulate the questions that we would like to put to this archive once it has been completed. I will address the formation of such a research agenda in the last chapter of this study.

In the meantime, one can make some observations on the general shape of these narratives based on the strong examples that have already appeared. I use the term *shape* purposefully. For if there is

Two Models of Holocaust Representation

one thing that we have learned from contemporary research in the humanities—the excess of jargon-laden theories aside—it is that all narratives, from the personal story to complex novels, are not simply naive and faithful transcriptions of experience but are built around preexisting armatures or schemata or master plots. New narratives may add to, play with, and subvert these story lines, but an appreciation of their uniqueness must begin with an understanding of the preexisting models. Certain of these models are "strong" models in the sense that Harold Bloom uses the term to designate works that exert a powerful influence on subsequent creativity.

In place of an overarching taxonomy of survivor narratives—which the state of the research does not at present permit—I will illustrate the differences among master, shaping Holocaust narratives by contrasting two examples: Elie Wiesel's *Night* and David Weiss Halivni's *The Book and the Sword*.[31] *Night* is probably the most influential survivor narrative. A short, accessible, and powerfully written narrative, *Night* was published in English in 1960 at the dawn of Holocaust consciousness in America, which in turn it helped to create. The book's influence was enhanced by the fame of its author, the paradigmatic survivor in our culture, and his increasing visibility in American public life. David Weiss Halivni is a renowned professor of Talmud who spent most of his adult life on the faculty of the Jewish Theological Seminary before leaving to teach at Columbia University when the seminary decided to ordain women rabbis. He published *The Sword and the Book* in 1996 after a distinguished record of scholarly publications on the development of the corpus of talmudic literature.

The books are admittedly different in significant ways. Their appearance is separated by thirty-five years; one is the work of a young man, the other the work of an older man; one is written in French, the other in English; one belongs to the category of serious literature, while the other presents itself only as a straightforward personal account. The reason for comparing them lies in a biographical connection that is more than accidental. Both Wiesel

Two Models of Holocaust Representation

and Halivni were born to religious families at about the same time in the Transylvanian city of Sighet, and they both emerged from boyhood to adolescence as promising, full-time students of the Talmud. Lest nostalgia should suffuse the sense of the past, it should be remembered that this vocation was becoming a rare one in a rapidly secularizing and urbanizing East European Jewish community that had been ravished by World War I.

Yet despite this common background, Wiesel and Halivni shape their stories in profoundly different ways. *Night* has become the classic narrative of rupture. It tells the story of how the spiritual world of such a youth is brutalized and broken down in the death camps. At the center of the narrative is the horrendous scene in which the camp inmates are forced to watch the hanging of a young boy who dies slowly on the gallows because his light weight will not bring his death agony to a quick end. To the question, "Where is God now?" a voice within the narrator answers: "Here He is—He is hanging here on this gallows." When the book concludes three days after the liberation of Buchenwald, the narrator looks at himself in a mirror for the first time since the ghetto; from the depths of the mirror he sees a corpse gazing back at him. Though his first work, *Night* remains Wiesel's most powerfully influential writing because early on it established a norm for what a Holocaust memoir should be. The defining moment is one of negative transformation. In the face of unspeakable horrors, the spiritual and cognitive identity of the victim breaks down leading to the death of the self. In later autobiographical works, Wiesel brings his narrator into the postwar world and delineates a portrait of the survivor as a man who is living a kind of death in life and who is possessed by the burden of bearing witness to the catastrophe.

In *The Book and the Sword* Halivni stakes out a very different claim as to what a Holocaust memoir can be. He is interested less in representing the destruction of identity—and all the horrors that accompany it—than in the persistence of identity. The reason Halivni devotes the preponderance of his book to his life before the

Two Models of Holocaust Representation

war and to his life after the war is because of the essential and deep-running continuity between the two, which revolves around his vocation as a student of the Talmud. There are differences, to be sure. He studies Talmud differently now than he did then, and he is burdened by fears and insecurities he ascribes to the trauma of the war. But the central axis of identity remains unbroken.

The strength of this axis is underscored by the one, brief section of the book that deals with events that transpired during the Holocaust itself. (The very paucity of material on the author's time in the camps makes a statement about the relative importance of before and after and during, and it will make the book a disappointment to connoisseurs of atrocity.) Halivni had been transferred to a slave labor camp whose inmates dug tunnels to protect future munitions factories from Allied bombardment. Every night he would pass by a Nazi guard eating a greasy sandwich; one night the grease had made the paper the sandwich was wrapped in translucent, and Halivni was able to make out that the paper was actually a page torn out of a Jewish legal code. It was, he writes,

> a page of *Orach Chaim,* a volume of the *Shulhan Aruch,* Pesil Balaban's edition. The Balabans began publishing the *Shulhan Aruch,* the Jewish Code of Law, in Lemberg in 1839. The first publisher was Abraham Balaban, and after his death he was succeeded by his widow, Pesil. Pesil's edition of the *Shulhan Aruch* was the best; it had all the commentaries. . . . As a child of a poor but scholarly home, I had always wanted to have her edition. . . . Here, of all places, in the shadows of the tunnel, under the threatening gaze of the German, a page from [Pesil's] *Shulhan Aruch,* fatty spots all over it, met my eyes.[32]

The paper is coaxed from the hands of the guard and becomes a focus of clandestine study and a rallying point for the religious prisoners. This vignette, which is quite beautifully told, does not come across as pious preening; rather, it serves to reveal an unexpungeable connection between the boy and the young man, even under the most unspeakable conditions. The point of the passage is not the appalling sacrilege of the greasy wurst wrapped in the sacred text but rather the young prisoner's familiar, almost caressing intimacy with the text and with its printing history and his excitement over this most peculiar fulfillment of a boyhood wish.

To say that Halivni's faith and vocation survived the nightmare of the Holocaust largely intact is not to say that he is more worthy than others who experienced and wrote about the same events differently. But he may be more representative. There are many survivors who struggled to establish lives after the war that are not the same as but are continuous with the religious, political, or cultural or even family values they held before the war. This is especially true in the case of the enormous expansion of Orthodox Jewish life and institutions in Israel and America, which could not have taken place if survivors and their communities had focused on the devastation caused by the Holocaust rather than on restoring what had been lost. Such survivors are more numerous than we think, and their stories have much to teach us, even if they run counter to the grain of our received notions of what it means to have survived the Holocaust.

Survivors' experiences are varied, yet the dominance of the exceptionalist model led to our recouping their narratives under the sign of rupture. The widespread phenomenon of continuity has been underrepresented and underreported. Continuity does not mean sameness, nor is it necessarily a product of repression, denial, and emotional constriction. Reconstructing a life after the war and striving to incorporate in that new life elements of prewar identity and belief deserve to be seen as a struggle as dramatic as the struggle to survive in the camps, in hiding, or in the forests during the war. To take the reconstructed life seriously does not mean to minimize the infinite suffering that preceded it nor the unending effects of that suffering. What it does ask us to do is to attend to the matrix of identity and society into which the survivor was born and to examine the reconstructed life in relationship not only to the common trauma that intervened but also to the formation of the life that came before.

The sites of the fourth area at issue are at once more institutional and pragmatic: universities and museums. Among the questions that arise out of the milieu of the academy are these: What is the essential canon of Holocaust literature? What should be the curriculum in the undergraduate classroom? Where should the study of the Holocaust be located among the departments and disciplines of the university? And, given the institutional organization of knowledge, how should graduate students of the Holocaust be trained? When it comes to museum work and the work of museums there is a similar set of crucial determinations: How is the presentation of the Holocaust affected by the community of visitors served by the museum? Does the Holocaust stand alone or is it to be related to the catastrophes of other peoples? How are the events of 1939–45 to be connected to the substance of Jewish history before and after? In the economy of representation, what are the claims made by the inner experience of the victims on the visually forceful culture of the Nazi perpetrators?

These are issues of such enormous import that each deserves the kind of careful consideration that is not possible within the compass of this inquiry. It will be enough to sketch along general lines the contrastive approaches to these matters suggested by the constructivist and exceptionalist models. For even though these are pragmatic determinations, there is a crucial question of principle that arises from the application of the two models: Can they be harmonized, the one complementing the other, or are they ultimately at odds with one another? I limit my observations to literary and cultural works relating to the Holocaust, although the issues are similar in the case of history and thought.

For the constructivist model, of course, context is paramount. The language a story or poem is written in—or in the case of film,

Two Models of Holocaust Representation

music, or art the appropriate semiotic code—is a key factor in understanding how a work summons up and breaks with the practices of the past under the pressure of the catastrophe. Of central concern will be how writing in Italian, French, Polish, and German plays with and against the cultural trends and preoccupations in those language cultures. There will also be a critical differentiation between literary works written in Jewish languages (Hebrew and Yiddish) and European languages; this is a distinction that bears on the issue not only of cultural repertoire but also of audience. Who can and who will read the text, whether it is during the event or in its aftermath? When it comes to training scholars and teachers, it therefore stands to reason that students should have a grounding in the Jewish languages of the Jewish victims and in one or more of the European languages in which they spoke and wrote. Familiarity with language implies by extension familiarity with the culture, history, and religious texts of these societies. This necessary mastery of specific context applies as well to the study of the reception of Holocaust works after the war because the dynamic of memory and denial is decisively shaped by conditions of national culture. For all these reasons, entities such as departments, programs, and centers of "Holocaust studies"—as opposed to the study of the Holocaust within departments of Jewish studies, German literature, English literature, and so forth—carry the danger of discouraging students from the hard work of making themselves at home in the foreign-language cultures in which the works of Holocaust culture were mostly created.

In the case of museums, the constructivist premise underscores the importance of the community, in the widest sense of the term, in which the museum is located. The Yad Vashem Memorial Museum in Jerusalem and the U.S. Holocaust Memorial Museum in Washington may reasonably shape their exhibitions differently because of the divergent populations they serve and because of their role in the formation of the collective memory of different national communities. Museums in America may in fact serve multiple and overlapping communities—say, for example, a museum under Jewish sponsorship that is regularly visited by groups of public-school children—yet the ultimate questions will remain the same: How can the Holocaust be presented in a way that is relevant to the lives of the museum's visitors? A key determination is whether the Holocaust is placed in the context of Jewish history—the classical culture of Ashkenazic Jewry before the war and the state of Israel afterward, for example—or whether the time frame is limited to the rise of Nazism and the war years.

The exceptionalist model recommends a very different conception of the museum. Public relations and pedagogics, though necessary, remain secondary to the mission of creating an unflinching encounter with the horror of the Holocaust. The museum traduces its purpose when it adjusts the meaning of the Holocaust to fit the needs of group or national identity formation. The "meaning" of the Holocaust is, in an absolute sense, its own memory, and this is the memory of an event that, despite the multiple contexts that help to illuminate it, stands beyond those contexts in a space of its own. The job of the museum is difficult and austere, for it must encourage an encounter with an event that repels and offers no message of deliverance.

In university study, the exceptionalist model focuses on a canon of works whose intelligibility is guaranteed by reference to a shared event. Because that event is unprecedented in its extremity, the works that represent the Holocaust owe more to each other and to the special discourse that has arisen around the catastrophe than they do to preexistent literary and cultural traditions. As a literary canon, Holocaust literature has its own "poetics," a set of internal rules and strategies that produce its meaning. Graduate training would therefore aim at equipping scholars and teachers with a knowledge of all aspects of this Holocaust discourse. Just as the Nazi genocide sucked all the Jews of Europe into the ovens regardless of whether they were religious, Zionist, or acculturated or whether they were from Paris, Czernowitz, or Soliniki, so too the Holocaust deserves to be studied on its own terms, not because of reverential piety for the event, but because it is more profoundly understood in terms of itself. When it comes to studying the refractions of the Holocaust in contemporary life and popular culture, the job of the scholar and critic is to plot and expose the divergence of these media representations from the grim reality of the way things really were.

The obvious question is why can there not be a fruitful synthesis between these two approaches? When there are two models, each of which has its strengths and insights to offer, cannot the two be combined to create a more powerful framework of understanding? My answer to this question is a qualified yes; yet the accompanying qualifications, which have to do with balance and appropriateness, are not insubstantial. Certainly not all Holocaust literature depends upon a density of cultural reference to be properly understood. There is, for example, a whole category of writings by Jewish women with Aryan looks and good German who survived and wrote fiction, poetry, and memoirs in adopted languages that constitutes what can truly be called a displaced literature. It is about this kind of writing that the exceptionalist model and its applied methods have the most illuminating things to say. The more a writer is uprooted and displaced, generally speaking, the more his or her work will be pulled into the centripetal orbit of the Holocaust conceived of as a universe unto itself. Yet even here, as we saw in the case of the literature of the concentration camps, the lens of culture that frames the victims' experiences is never entirely absent. In fact, in the corpus of Holocaust literature in its entirety, I would submit, the number of works in which culture and context are not central is relatively small.

But corpus, in the end, is not canon. The canon of Holocaust literature, the subset of works that are regarded as the most effective representations of the event, has been determined in large measure by the dominance of the exceptionalist model, which in turn has shaped popular and critical taste. Now, there is nothing improper or

Two Models of Holocaust Representation

conspiratorial about this dominance, and its sway can be explained by a number of historical factors that were discussed at the beginning of this study. Yet the results have at times been unfortunate. A case in point is the neglect of the vast and illuminating literature from the ghettos of occupied Eastern Europe in favor of concentration camp narratives. The advantages of utilizing both the constructivist and exceptionalist models in tandem are obvious. But this kind of synthesis works only if deployed with a critical balance and openness in which the nature of the work being examined dictates the combination of methods to be brought into play. Until recently, however, the constructivist model as an explanatory framework has been given short shrift. This has made it difficult to achieve critical balance and openness and has in turn affected the body of materials that make up the Holocaust canon.

The resistance to the constructivist-contextualist model has been of two sorts. In their austere focus on the horror of the Holocaust taken on its own terms, writers like Lawrence Langer have made a principled argument for the exceptionality of the event and the consequent responsibility of the critic-scholar to descend into the abyss of the concentrationary universe. There is nothing indulgent or mitigating about this descent, and few can sustain the rigors of this high calling. There are others, however, for whom the self-contained conception of the Holocaust serves as a license rather than a discipline. It is easier to tell yourself that despite the critical diversity of Holocaust texts, written in a variety of languages but given in English translation, little of essence has been lost. It is easier to master the radically simple and impoverished vocabulary of the concentration camps than to acquire a familiarity with the complex cultural milieus from which the victims were snatched up, whether it is a Russian shtetl, Weimar Frankfurt, or interwar Lodz. And it is easier still to create a canon of works whose analysis does not require the interpreter to catch the kind of ironic allusions to Jewish classical literature that were second nature to texts' authors and implied audience.

The resistance to foreign matters and foreign languages is, of course, notoriously American and is in no sense special to the reception of the Holocaust. As Americans, we fully expect alien cultures to present themselves to us in intelligible form, and we resent being called upon to take what we consider extraordinary measures to understand documents that should, or eventually will, be available to us in translation if they are genuinely important. To the extent that this impatience is a native trait, it too plays a role in the complex process of the "Americanization" of the Holocaust, which is the fifth and final topic of this chapter.

That the Holocaust has been Americanized, by which I mean refracted through means of representation that are characteristic of American culture, is a fact that is beyond discussion. In chapter 1, we surveyed the American terms on which the Holocaust was admitted to these shores and absorbed over time into the folds of public discourse and popular culture. The question is not whether this phenomenon has taken place but what is one's stance toward it. It is here that the exceptionalist and constructivist models square off. If the differences between the two in the discussion above have sometimes been subtle, the lines are drawn much more starkly when it comes to the representation of the Holocaust in America. And it is little wonder, for as time passes, the authors of the stories, memoirs, film scripts, and plays are increasingly less likely to have been witnesses, or even the sons and daughters of witnesses, to the catastrophe and their works correspondingly more dependent on the mediation of the imagination.

For the critic writing under the sign of the exceptionalist model the task of criticism is to plot the divergence between the American appropriations of the Holocaust and the Holocaust "the way it was." What is difficult for all people is especially difficult for Americans: to abide the horror without appeal to forms of amelioration or redemption. The temptation to vulgarization is nearly insuperable. In Langer's *Art from the Ashes,* for example, the bar is set too high. There is no American writing included at all, except for an essay by Elie Wiesel; the only document written in English is an excerpt from

Two Models of Holocaust Representation

Christopher Browning's work on the mobile killing squads in the East. Under the exceptionalist model, the task of analysis overlaps with a burden of responsibility that is at once moral and prophetic. It is the difficult job of the critic to assume the role of the mourner at the wedding, the truth teller who continually insists on our being suspicious of the purposes for the Holocaust being enlisted and remaining mindful of the gap between the latest celebrated refashioning of the Holocaust and the unspeakable reality of what actually took place.

For the constructivist model, the Americanization of the Holocaust is the scene of an endlessly fascinating intellectual drama whose subject is admittedly less the Holocaust than American culture. At the center of the drama is the spectacle of a formidable cultural system struggling with a tragic event alien to its nature and proceeding through stages of denial to an accommodation with the event on its own terms. It is axiomatic in this conception that the Holocaust will always be enlisted for ulterior purposes and that the destruction of European Jewry will always be perceived through an American lens and represented through styles of the imagination and modes of cultural production at work in our society. Here, too, there is room for judgment—though not endemic outrage—and for aesthetic discriminations between successful and unsuccessful works. There is admittedly much Holocaust art produced in America that should indeed be called vulgar, but its Americanness is not necessarily the ingredient responsible for its vulgarity. A novel like Philip Roth's *The Ghost Writer,* whose theme is precisely the exploitation of the moral prerogatives of Holocaust memory by a young writer making his career, might be praised for its ironic awareness of how the Holocaust is used, while at the same time William Styron's novel *Sophie's Choice* might be faulted for invoking a similar theme with self-aggrandizement rather than critical self-awareness.

There is surely room for both of these models in studying the reception of the Holocaust in America, and our understanding is richer for the interplay between the two perspectives. Yet in my own

Two Models of Holocaust Representation

practice as a student of the Americanization of the Holocaust, I find the constructivist model to have a greater intellectual yield. The prophetic admonitions of the exceptionalist position have permanently lodged in the background of my mind, and they bid me never to lose sight of the irreparable horror and the extremity of human abasement. But as a mission and critical occupation, the continual tracking of the betrayals of this standard strikes me as an endeavor of limited possibilities. I therefore prefer to focus on the way the Holocaust is being constructed out of American materials.

Works of popular culture, especially movies, have played a signal role in the Americanization of the Holocaust. I argued in chapter 1 that it was cultural products of this sort that caused the Holocaust to leap from the bounded concerns of one religious-ethnic community into the public arena of the American nation as a whole. As an illustration of this argument, I offer in the next chapter a discussion of three Hollywood films: *Judgment at Nuremberg, The Pawnbroker,* and *Schindler's List.* There are, to be sure, other, independent, non-commercial, and documentary films that deal with the Holocaust more persuasively, and there are other commercial films that touch on the Holocaust partially or obliquely. But I would submit that it is these three American-made, studio-backed feature films that have contributed the most to the wider dissemination of the Holocaust in the American popular mind.

The status of these studies as illustrations needs to be underscored. This book makes no pretense to being a history of the reception of the Holocaust in American popular culture. Such a project would be of much greater scope and would give abundant attention to the Anne Frank diary, especially in its stage and screen versions, William Styron's novel *Sophie's Choice* (as well as the film), the television miniseries *Holocaust,* Art Spiegelman's *Maus,* and other key points of development. While the three Hollywood films are important in themselves, I mean for these discussions to serve as illustrations of a general way of working with popular cultural materials relating to the Holocaust. My purpose has not been to approach these films from the point of view of film studies or film criticism, nor to offer a formal analysis of how they work as films, nor has it been to give a literary critical analysis of their themes and structures. Rather, I've sought to discover what these movies meant to their viewers when they first appeared and how that meaning strikes us now. My sights have been fixed on the issues current in American culture that make the Holocaust imaginable and admissible in certain shapes and guises, while at the same time I have endeavored to appreciate the particular alchemy of each film. I have not tried to conceal my own judgments, which are roughly typical of the Jewish academic mandarin class to which I belong; yet my object has been to understand the assumptions underlying the popular debates and critical discourse that surrounded these films.

The larger purpose of this exercise is to increase the measure of self-awareness we bring to the shaping of Holocaust memory in America. The future of that memory is the subject of this volume's concluding chapter.

3

The Holocaust at the Movies:
Three Studies in Reception

JUDGMENT AT NUREMBERG (1961)

The concentration camp newsreel footage, lasting seven minutes, shown two-thirds of the way through Stanley Kramer's 1961 film *Judgment at Nuremberg* was a scandal that American viewers were apparently willing to put up with. Similar footage, shot by the U.S. Army Signal Corps upon the liberation of the camps, had been screened in American movie houses immediately after the war, where it preceded the main feature rather than being part of it.[1] Incorporated in the miscellaneous war news about the allied victory, those celluloid images of horror had soon faded from public consciousness. Hollywood had ceased the vast production of patriotic World War II pictures that had been geared to entertain and to serve; the Cold War had made allies of the Germans, and war movies, like *The Young Lions* (1958), now tended to condemn war and stress the suffering on both sides. It is in the 1959 film version of the enormously successful stage adaptation of Anne Frank's diary that the genocide of European Jewry is placed for the first time before a general American film audience, although the film labors mightily to protect its viewers from a vivid intimation of what Anne's fate will be after her capture.[2]

Given the gruesome nature of these images, all the more unexpected because they are infiltrated within the gloss of a big-budget

The Holocaust at the Movies

Hollywood movie, one might have expected contemporary audiences to register shock and consternation. Yet reviews of the film—whether in national magazines, film journals, or intellectual monthlies—make almost no reference to the footage.[3] Apart from assessing the production and its performances, critical discussion centers on the question of the collective responsibility of the German people for the crimes of Nazism, a question that had been vehemently debated during the war-crimes trials right after the war but had slipped from public awareness until *Judgment at Nuremberg* dramatically brought it back to life.

This avoidance of atrocity is not simply moral callowness but a response encouraged by the equivocal uses to which the newsreel footage is put by the producer and director, Stanley Kramer. On the one hand, Kramer uses a quick jolt of horror to get us to acknowledge the unprecedented enormity of the crimes committed by the Germans. Yet once he has accomplished this goal, he does everything possible to lead us away from our revulsion and the troubling questions it raises, and instead he points us in the direction of the grander and more universalist themes of collective and individual responsibility for the evil that humans visit on other human beings. In the narrative accompanying the footage, the prosecutor blunts the horror by effacing the identity of the bulldozed corpses, describing them vaguely as coming from every occupied country in Europe. When the footage is over, the scene cuts abruptly to the prison mess, where one of the defendants, a former judge, declares that the unspeakable things he has seen in the films must have been fabricated because they could never have taken place. From the prison the film jumps to a *Bierstube,* where the senior American judge, Dan Haywood, is having a drink with the aristocratic widow of an executed German general, played by Marlene Dietrich. She is outraged that he should entertain the thought that people like her and her husband knew about the concentration camps; and he counters by observing dryly that as far as he can tell no one in all of Germany seems to have known about them. Thus a shocking encounter with evil of unfathomable proportions is soon stabilized and contained by shifting the focus to the question of blame and putting the viewer at a safe distance of judgment from those who refuse to accept responsibility.

But our safety is not so easily assured. Although the syntax of the film rushes away from the horror, there are subtle effects that force us to linger and remain exposed to the images before our eyes. Instead of rolling the footage without interruption, Kramer continually cuts back and forth from the film to the faces of the principal participants in the courtroom drama as they register the images projected on the screen before them. There is the bug-eyed astonishment of one of the lesser defendants; there is the solemn, riveted glare of Ernst Janning, the former German minister of justice, played by Burt Lancaster; there is the tight scowl of disdain worn by the defense counsel, played by Maximilian Schell; and, finally, there is the face of Spencer Tracy, who plays Judge Haywood.

In a film composed almost entirely of close-up head shots, Tracy's face stands out. Sitting across from one another in the beer hall, Tracy's and Dietrich's faces are a study in contrasts. Her face, plangent in a softly lit chiaroscuro, is a composition of smooth ovals of cheekbones, eyes, and mouth. The almond-shaped eyes under perfectly drawn brows look directly at her interlocutor with a mixture of assertion and supplication. When she speaks a beguiling shadow calls attention to the height of her cheekbones and the fragile flute of her nostrils. Tracy's face is another continent altogether. It is a rugged terrain of ridges and grooves. The narrow eyes, set deeply in their sockets, are ringed by pouches beneath and networks of crinkles to the side. The nearly invisible eyebrows disappear into still deeper furrows. For the sake of a courtly compliment, the wrinkles momentarily dispose themselves into a charming mask before falling back into a physiognomy of distress.

It is upon this face that the camera lingers while the concentration camp footage is being projected in the courtroom. While a single fleeting glimpse suffices to register the reactions of the other

Judge Haywood (Spencer Tracy) views concentration camp newsreel footage at the Nuremberg trial. *Judgment at Nuremberg*. United Artists

Playing the widow of an executed Wehrmacht general, Marlene Dietrich defends the honor of decent Germans to Judge Haywood. *Judgment at Nuremberg*

players, the face of the aging judge is returned to repeatedly. Lit by a flickering projector against the darkened room, his face fills the entire frame. As the prosecutor's voice lectures incessantly, the camera alternates between the naked corpses and the judge's face. Our attention is focused on the mouth. The eyes are withdrawn behind horn-rimmed spectacles, and the nose seems flatter and more stolid. It is the mouth that goes through a series of contortions. First the lips are tightly compressed so that the mouth disappears and becomes only a blank point at which all the creased lines meet. Then the mouth opens in a reflex of revulsion, and a hand appears to cover the mouth as if to suppress a wave of nausea. When the camera returns, the hand is gone and the mouth is closed again. A dry swallow follows a subtle grinding of the jaws.

What is revealed in the pained topography of Spencer Tracy's face is a knowledge that is articulated nowhere else in *Judgment at Nuremberg*. After administrating a dose of atrocity with this film-within-a-film, Stanley Kramer proceeds to use it largely as a shorthand symbol ("the camps") for the enormity of the crimes the Germans are now so eager to distance themselves from. Beyond the prosecutor's dry recitation of the brute facts, no one inside or outside the courtroom endeavors to understand or interpret or respond to what the film has disclosed. This is not because the horror is so unspeakably beyond analysis and explanation; this may be true, but it is not Kramer's motive. He wishes to shock his audience—and perhaps to garner some moral prestige from being the first to dare to do what he has done—and then move the film back to the higher and more stable ground occupied by questions of justice and responsibility. Because the film declines to dramatize substantive responses to the images of genocide within its own artifice, it is little wonder, then, that contemporary viewers and reviewers fail to take notice as well.

To be sure, Spencer Tracy's understated grimaces do not add up to a substantive grappling with the reality of atrocity; but they do reflect a subverbal, affective knowledge that is singular in the film. It is a knowledge that is easy to miss on first viewing because of the sensational nature of the footage and because of the grander questions of principle that are immediately set before us. Here is a good man, a judge from the backwoods of Maine, whose craggy face reflects long experience with the misdeeds of men and women and the heavy burden of judgment. Yet what his eyes are taking in as the images flicker on the screen is evidence of an evil that transcends his experience and imagination. He is an American in the throes of discovering a monstrous horror that lies outside the orbit of American experience and imagination. The German characters in the film, whether the defendants at the bar or the "ordinary" Germans, seem to know all about it, although they cover it up with various postures of avoidance or denial. The Americans, even the unrelenting prosecutor, have given themselves over to the task of fixing guilt and passing judgment. It is only Tracy's Judge Haywood who is surprised in the act of discovering and absorbing this terrible knowledge.

There is one more figure in the courtroom whose stunned reaction to the footage is momentarily captured by the camera. This is an African-American GI, who is part of a contingent of guards, all the rest white, who stand rigidly at attention behind the defendants and at the entrance to the courtroom. The footage includes pictures of the corpses of young children, and the prosecutor's narrative explains that the Nazis would kill the children by hanging and then would suspend their bodies on hooks like pictures on a wall. At this point the camera cuts for two or three seconds to the face of the black soldier, whose usual demeanor of professional impassivity is interrupted by the look of lost astonishment in his eyes. The message is clear: When it comes to killing the innocent by hanging, America's own record is not without blemish. This is one of several allusions to morally problematic episodes in American history; the defense counsel brandishes Oliver Wendell Holmes's approval of sterilizing the mentally incompetent and points to the bombing of Hiroshima and Nagasaki.

These references do not set up a moral equivalence between Germany and America, but they do highlight a reflexive movement in

The Holocaust at the Movies

the film. Although they sit in judgment, the Americans are themselves not beyond judgment. The exercise of justice is everywhere
and always exposed to the pressures of expediency, as Judge Haywood
discovers when he and his colleagues are told by senators and generals that it is not in America's interest to alienate the German people
by handing down severe sentences. The pressures are resisted, and
in the end justice is done; and in its confirmation of the possibility
of American justice *Judgment at Nuremberg* is located at an enormous
distance from the grim self-lacerations of *The Pawnbroker*, a film that
appeared only four years later. Yet at the same time, there is no escape
from the fact that an examination of the German war crimes
inevitably provokes self-examination. Or, to put it another way, the
horrors of the war in Europe compel our interest only to the degree
to which they tell us something about who we are as Americans.

Taken as a whole, then, *Judgment at Nuremberg* is a film in which
three different stories are told. The first and most manifest is a story
about the submission of the German people, especially its professional classes, to the Nazi madness and the denial of responsibility
for this willing compliance. The second is an implicit story about the
majesty of American justice—as well as its vulnerabilities—as a moral
yardstick for understanding human affairs. The third is a buried story
about the visceral discovery both of the horror of the Holocaust and
of the fascination exerted by the evil of its perpetrators. All three of
these stories were involved in the clamorous reception the movie
received when it first appeared in 1961, as they are today when we
view it with the saturated erudition that is inevitably our possession
in an era after the rise of Holocaust literature, Holocaust studies, and
Holocaust museums. What has changed in our perception of the film,
I would offer, is that what was most hidden when the film appeared
strikes us today as most evident, and what was most evident then
now seems less compelling.

When *Judgment at Nuremberg* was first screened on December 14,
1961, it was not just another movie premier but a major cultural
event. Kramer and United Artists staged the film's premier in the

The Holocaust at the Movies

Kongresshalle in the shadow of the Berlin Wall. The invited viewers were Allied commanders, members of the West German senate, and a planeload of journalists who had been flown in from the United States for the occasion. Willy Brandt, the mayor of West Berlin, opened the evening and addressed the overflowing audience as if on a state occasion.[4] The premier was anticipated by a feature story in *Life* magazine[5] and by a profile of Stanley Kramer in the magazine section of the *New York Times*.[6] The film was widely noticed, and later that spring Stanley Kramer, who had never before won an Oscar, was made the recipient of the Irving Thalberg Award of the Academy of Motion Picture Arts and Sciences. Although the award recognized Kramer generally for high-quality movie making, it was clear that the occasion had been his direction of *Judgment at Nuremberg*.

The film's celebrity—and perhaps the possibility of its having an audience altogether—was enhanced by the worldwide attention given to the trial of Adolf Eichmann, whose capture had been announced by the Israelis on May 24, 1960. During the course of 1961, the movie was being shot in Hollywood as Eichmann was being tried in Jerusalem. For Murray Schumach, writing in the *New York Times*, the parallels between the two trials were worth noting:

> In a somber courtroom set in Hollywood, genocide is as current these days as it is in the Beit Haam, in Jerusalem, where Adolf Eichmann is being tried for responsibility for the deaths of six million Jews. In Hollywood, however, cameras and actors are working in a replica of the courtroom of Nuremberg, where civilized nations set the legal precedent that made a special crime of genocide.[7]

Judgment at Nuremberg, then, is not just another Hollywood entertainment but a celluloid replica of the original war crimes proceedings that created the law under which Eichmann was then being tried. The Eichmann trial was everywhere in the news and public discussion during that year, and it was the general currency of such issues

The Holocaust at the Movies

as individual responsibility for state-sponsored genocide that allowed Kramer to gain a mainstream audience for his film. He made what use of the trial he could. According to *Time* magazine's caustic observation, Kramer went so far as to "shrewdly time the release of this movie to coincide with the reading of the judgment in the trial of Adolf Eichmann."[8]

To be fair, the idea for the movie had preceded the trial. Already in 1957 the movie's screenwriter, Abby Mann, had begun to write the script for a television drama on the Nuremberg trials that was broadcast in 1959 as part of the Playhouse 90 series. (The producer was Harry Brodkin, who produced the television miniseries *Holocaust* in 1978.[9]) The later use made of the Eichmann trial is just another aspect of what some called Stanley Kramer's astuteness and others called his commercialism. Kramer was known in Hollywood in the late fifties as the master of the "message movie," a film that addressed a large and serious issue and at the same time was commercially successful. In the three years before *Judgment at Nuremberg* he had produced and directed *The Defiant Ones*, whose subject is racial intolerance, *On the Beach*, which addresses the aftermath of global nuclear war, and *Inherit the Wind*, which is an account of a schoolteacher's trial for teaching evolution in a southern town. The Nazi genocide was therefore part of a natural progression of engaging controversial issues. Concerning the aims of his filmmaking, Kramer professes that "[I] want to provoke an audience into thought. . . . That's about as much as I can accomplish, but that's a great deal. It isn't necessary for people to agree with me. It is enough just to open up the gate of thought and controversy."[10] For observers of the Hollywood scene—that is, observers inured to the general run of entertainments being served up during that period—Kramer is a special instance, an insider who has "a penchant for dealing with bold, unconventional, nonconformist, and uncompromising themes."[11] In the case of *Judgment at Nuremberg*, Kramer was generally applauded, even by those who faulted the realization of the film, for presenting his audience with large and difficult issues and making them think.

The Holocaust at the Movies

Given that the motion-picture industry was dismayed at the prospect of presenting any controversial subject matter, Kramer's courage looms even larger. After giving the film an admiring review in the daily paper, Bosley Crowthers, the *New York Times* film critic, wrote an article in the Sunday arts section that expresses a kind of communal debt of gratitude to Stanley Kramer, because "he plainly intended this drama to excite contemporary thought and give us a little elevation for reflecting on some problems of our times."[12]

A little elevation was no small accomplishment in those times. Kramer's secret formula for making big issues pay at the box office proved to be simple enough: hire big stars and cast some of them radically against type. Celebrity guarantees a mass audience, and the perverse casting creates interest and even notoriety. The cast of *On the Beach*, for example, included Gregory Peck, Ava Gardner, Fred Astaire, and Anthony Perkins; it cast Ava Gardner as an unglamorous woman who "has lived too long and drunk too much" and Fred Astaire as a scientist who "neither sings a note nor dances a step."[13] Kramer repeated the formula for *Judgment at Nuremberg*. The film's pantheon includes Spencer Tracy, Marlene Dietrich, Burt Lancaster, Richard Widmark, Maximilian Schell, Judy Garland, and Montgomery Clift. The notion of an ensemble of stars is formalized in the film's logo, which shows the silhouetted profiles of these seven actors gazing in the same direction; the logo is screened for a considerable interval both at the opening of the film and at its close, while a series of rousing German marches is sung by an unseen military chorus. Tracy and Dietrich were given roles that were roughly continuous with the personae that had attached to them during their long careers in motion pictures. Schell, a relative newcomer to Hollywood who was better known as the younger brother of Maria Schell, was given a part that well suited his German accent and mercurial appearance. Richard Widmark, however, is plucked from hardboiled crime films and made into a righteous prosecutor of alleged Nazi war criminals. Judy Garland, a singer-actress with a fanatical following, had not appeared in a film in six years and was cast as a diffident heavy-set housewife who as a teenager had been involved in a famous trial based on the Nazi race laws. The greatest tension between star and role is reserved for Burt Lancaster, who had long played virile, charismatic, and rhetorically powerful figures. Kramer casts him as the chief defendant, Ernst Janning, a distinguished jurist who had cooperated with the Nazis. For most of the film he is required to sit silent and expressionless, refusing to communicate with his counsel and spurning contact with his codefendants.

In the contemporary reception of the film, Kramer's star formula garnered very mixed responses. For some the very conception opened itself to ridicule. Brendan Gill in the *New Yorker* observes that the film threatens at times to turn into a "judicial Grand Hotel."[14] In *Film Quarterly* Gavin Lampert wickedly derides Kramer for mounting an "All-Star Concentration Camp Drama, with Special Guest Victim Appearances,"[15] a line that Pauline Kael takes up with special delight in her essay on Kramer. Most reviewers, however, discriminated more respectfully among the stars, and many singled out Tracy's and Schell's performances for praise. According to *Commonweal*, for example, Tracy's understated authority allows him to turn in a "magnificent performance as an intensely sincere man searching for answers."[16] Schell's "quasi-neurotic fervor" is thought to be a good match for the moral ambiguities of the defense's case. Montgomery Clift's portrayal of a laborer who was sterilized under the Nuremberg Laws is widely admired for its edgy and idiosyncratic dramatic intensity, although the rationale for the part is questioned altogether. Judy Garland plays a woman who was befriended as a girl by an older Jewish man who was convicted on false charges of having had sexual relations with her and was subsequently executed. Yet despite the overwhelming pathos with which she plays the role, the persistence of her identity as a singer and as a child star cannot be put away. As Stanley Kauffmann writes in the *New Republic*, "Miss Garland is a popular singer with a fanatical following. The attempt to treat her here as a great actress who has graciously condescended to a minor role is inappropriate."[17]

The Holocaust at the Movies

In the cases of Marlene Dietrich and Burt Lancaster, the familiarity they bring with them to the film presents even greater difficulties, but for opposite reasons. Dietrich is cast too close to type, and the type is inseparably fused with her own aura as an icon who had long played seductive, worldly women with languorous eyes and a sibilant German accent. As the aristocratic widow of an executed German general, the type is socially enhanced and played with an "alluring hauteur."[18] Yet the care given to lighting her magnificent face and the handsome and stylized outfits in which she is dressed—and this amid the rubble of bombed-out and impoverished Nuremberg—make it clear that here is a personality that is visiting this picture from elsewhere.[19] Burt Lancaster, on the other hand, is required by his role to do exactly what is least characteristic of his cinematic persona: to sit still and keep his mouth shut. In ashen makeup, he "gives a somnabulistic, clench-jaw rendition of an eminent Nazi jurist. A glimpse of those gorgeous choppers might have helped," opined Ronald Steel drolly, reflecting the expectations that viewers had of Lancaster and the resulting sense of disorientation.[20] "He could not have been more wrongly cast, or more absurdly directed," asserts Arthur B. Clark. "Our first sight of him makes us suspect something is wrong with him; his bearing throughout the trial is almost catatonic; and, when he finally comes to life and speaks a piece for which the audience has not been prepared, he is unbelievable and embarrassing to watch."[21]

In commenting on the performances by Montgomery Clift and Judy Garland, *Variety* observes that "familiarity intrudes on the spectator's conscious [*sic*], and he has insufficient time to divorce actor from character," and suggests that "the roles might better have been handed to lesser-known players."[22] This is sensible counsel indeed, yet it is advice that Kramer could not have followed. He believed that without stars, and not just one or two stars but a galaxy of them, the American public could not be brought into the movie houses to confront this most difficult and ghastly subject. He further believed that the audience would be soothed by a veteran actor like

The Holocaust at the Movies

Spencer Tracy playing to his strengths and would be provoked and astonished to see other well-known actors giving supposedly virtuoso performances in unfamiliar roles. Kramer may indeed have had an astute sense of his audience, but he also had the grandiosity to think that he could have his cake and eat it too. He wanted to exploit the celebrity of famous actors and at the same time prevent the proprietary charisma of each of them from diverting from, and even masking, his high purpose.

What in the end *was* the high purpose of *Judgment at Nuremberg*? Ostensibly, the purpose of the film was to push viewers to open up old wounds and to face a question whose discussion in the current political and cultural climate was highly inconvenient: the enormity of German crimes and the responsibility for them on the part of Germans who were not among Hitler's inner circle. Yet despite the kudos accorded Kramer for his moral risk-taking, most intelligent contemporary comment on the film was not in fact stimulated or provoked to take on these issues. There are two basic directions in which reviewers preferred to take the discussion. In one case, the issue of German crimes was kicked upstairs, as it were, into the realm of higher principle, and in the other, it was kicked back into the American arena. In both cases, as we shall see, the evasion is one encouraged by the film itself.

Despite the importance accorded to the matter of German guilt, most writers on the film saw the issue's true significance in its serving as an instance of something larger and more important still. Brendan Gill, that most affable and worldly of *New Yorker* writers, justifies his praise for the film by averring that it transcends its time and its place.

> The questions are among the biggest that can be asked and are no less fresh and thrilling for being thousands of years old (and for having been tossed and gored in no telling how many millions of undergraduate bull sessions from Academe on); they concern nothing less than the degree of our accountability, individually and collectively,

as members of the human race, for the life and well-being of every other member of the race.[23]

The well-being of the entire human race is high moral ground indeed, and from those dizzying heights German crimes and German guilt attain their true function as illustrations of larger truths.

Writing in a *Commentary* symposium on the movie, Jason Epstein, the vice president of Random Books and the editor-in-chief of the Modern Library, sees in *Judgment at Nuremberg* something other than the thrill of tossing around great ideas. Epstein is one of the few writers on the film to explore the impact of Kramer's use of the concentration camp documentary footage. Rather than informing us about the nature of the German genocide—what a certain nation did to other specific peoples and nations—the footage forces us, in his view, to confront the frightening essence of twentieth-century politics. What happened in Germany was only a station in the unfolding of a dynamic of violence and mass death that has brought the world—the time is the height of the Cold War—to the brink of thermonuclear catastrophe. Hiroshima is the next station along this continuum, and the German defense counsel is not reticent about bringing it up. It is not with Spencer Tracy and the stern administration of American justice that Epstein identifies but with the undramatic complicity of the ordinary judges and lawyers who are on trial.

> It seems to me that we are being asked . . . to think of ourselves at the end of World War III in a position similar to that of the defendants—ordinary men . . . who under the stress of a national crisis are acquiescing in crimes beside which Hitler's will seem small. . . . [W]e too may one day be called to account for decisions we failed to make, for opportunities that we have overlooked, for alternatives we were too blind to know were there.[24]

From our vantage point, we recognize in Epstein's response the beginnings of a discourse that has become very familiar to us: the typological reading of the European Holocaust during World War II as an anticipation of the total nuclear holocaust to come.

The search for higher ground is encouraged by a basic structural problem in the film. The legal and moral premise of *Judgment at Nuremberg* is that because bureaucrats like the judges on trial acquiesced to the Nazi perversion of justice they are responsible for a system that led to the concentration camps, even though they were not directly involved in the implementation of the genocide. The problem lies in the gap between the results of the Final Solution, shown to us in the footage, and the lackluster judges in the dock. The two dramatic witnesses in the script—Rudolph Petersen, who had been sterilized (played by Montgomery Clift) and Irene Hoffman (played by Judy Garland), whose older Jewish friend was convicted of consorting with her and was executed for it—contribute very little to our understanding of the processes whereby ordinary Germans became complicit in genocide. The "nature of the crime for which the film finds them [the judges] guilty," writes Harris Dienstfrey in *Commentary*, "says nothing at all about either the causes of the development or the consequences of the Nazi period. There is a wide distance between a corrupt judiciary and the concentration camps. Yet at its end, the film acts as if it has satisfactorily fixed *all* its giant questions, not only the moral but the social and historical questions as well."[25] Stanley Kramer and Abby Mann, the scriptwriter, in fact evince almost no interest in tracing consequences and developments, in exploring how little things lead to big things, or in recreating the dense texture of historical change. It is precisely this vacancy that encourages viewers not to pause too long on the particulars and proceed directly to the broadest level of statement about the dilemmas of humankind.[26]

All of these efforts to delineate the "higher" relevance of the film's message are instances of universalization; and universalization is, without doubt, the most profound and pervasive mechanism by which the Holocaust was allowed entry into American culture, at the level of popular culture especially but at more exalted levels as well. Because of this dominance, it is worth looking more closely at what happens when the particularity of the Holocaust is universalized. Ever since the Enlightenment—and long before that in the medieval legacy of Greek philosophy—the universal has been privileged over the particular. To discern in a discrete institution, historical event, or cultural product a meaning that transcends the particular is to enhance the moral significance of the particular; it is, in a sense, to redeem the particular by rescuing it from its one-time, accidental and specific identity and then connecting it to a large order of value. In the case of the Holocaust, the historical significance of the event is supposedly elevated by virtue of its being taken as an example or illustration of a larger rubric such as the individual's responsibility for other human beings.

At the same time, universalizing is a way to avoid seeing the particular and what is troublingly un-universal about it. In *Judgment at Nuremberg*, for example, Kramer's screening of the concentration camp footage was applauded by some as an act of great moral courage. Yet although we are forced to look at the footage, we are not helped by the film to really see it. The footage is used as a sensational move to shock us into acknowledging the moral enormity of the crimes, but we are not asked to investigate their nature and genesis or to inquire about the identity of the victims. Nor are we given a framework in which to locate what we are watching. "The films themselves are the core of [the prosecutor's] argument," observed Ronald Steel.[27] In the absence of a true argument, our attention does not linger after the initial shock, and our outrage is available to be enlisted on behalf of the highest principles.

Universalization is, in the end, a double-edged sword. It evades its subject, on the one hand, yet on the other, it may, under certain conditions, represent the *only* way to approach the subject. The resistance to thinking about German responsibility for the Nazi genocide is, after all, one of the overt themes of *Judgment at Nuremberg*. During the thirteen years that intervene between the making of the movie and the time in which the action is set, the Cold War had become an

The Holocaust at the Movies

entrenched reality, and revisiting the culpability of the German allies for heinous crimes against humanity had become no more convenient later than it had been earlier. It is perhaps only a little surprising to hear the frank, monitory words of *Life Magazine* in the text accompanying a photo feature on the film: "Some who see the film will question the sense of reopening old wounds now, perhaps tending to estrange a free world ally and giving a propaganda wedge to the enemy."[28] In the face of the charge of giving comfort to the enemy, an inquiry into these troubling matters can march into American consciousness only if it is flying universal colors.

A related way of simultaneously seeing and not seeing is to make the German question into a reflection of American dilemmas. Aversive to focusing on shameful acts performed in foreign countries, American viewers could be persuaded to give their attention when there is a message about them as Americans. Whether this search for relevancy represents a courageous acceptance of self-exposure or an escape from gazing upon the anguished fate of others is, again, a critical ambiguity. We can say, perhaps, that it is a necessary and inevitable solipsism. In Abby Mann's script for *Judgment at Nuremberg* the references that reflect on American issues are explicitly flagged. There is the look on the face of the black soldier when hangings are mentioned. There is the opinion cited by the defense of Oliver Wendell Holmes approving sterilization for congenital feeblemindedness. There is the atomic bomb dropped on Hiroshima. Taken together, these references raise questions about the unassailability of American justice. The second half of the film drops the pretense of proving the case for legal responsibility and shifts to pressure on the court for light sentences exerted by American generals and senators on the eve of the Berlin airlift. The dramatic tension revolves not so much around the question of German guilt, which in a vague and muddled way is affirmed by the film, but around the question of American justice. Given public indifference to this late round of trials back home and given the official encouragement of leniency, will justice in fact be served?

The Holocaust at the Movies

While the reflexive focus of *Judgment at Nuremberg* is not lost on critics and reviewers, it is the producer/director himself who insistently promoted this approach to the film. While others spoke about implicit parallels and analogies to the American situation, Stanley Kramer gave interviews in which he vociferously stated that this in essence is what the film is really about.[29] In a major feature on Kramer in the Sunday magazine of the *New York Times* on the eve of the movie's premier, he has this to say about the film and himself:

> I am interested in the world and what we in America stand for. This interest is what attracted me to "Judgment at Nuremberg"—this concern for what we Americans stand for. I was not so much interested in what the Germans stood for, during the Hitler period or in the post-war years or now. It is not the attitude of the Germans that I have tried to emphasize in the film. It is the attitude of the Americans—the judge and the prosecuting attorney and all the others who participate in this necessarily fictionalized representation of the momentous judgments at Nuremberg."[30]

Viewing these statements from the vantage point of our media-conscious age, we are perfectly aware of what Kramer is up to: he is engaging in spin. He seeks to influence the reception of his new film and to encourage a conception of it as a work about our own attitudes as Americans rather than foreigners and their corruption; it is not about them, he insists, it is about us. Now, Kramer's call for a self-examination of our national moral fiber may be high-minded indeed, but it also expresses an anxiety about whether, in the eyes of American viewers, a film about foreign crimes will escape being off-putting.

While the producer/director has every right to promote his view of what the film is about, he surely has no monopoly. As an example of how the film was understood very differently by other viewers, I take the liberty of presenting a modest autobiographical recollection. It was the winter of ninth grade, my last year of junior

The Holocaust at the Movies

high school, when *Judgment at Nuremberg* came out, and I was taken along with my parents to see the film at the Poli Theater in Worcester, Massachusetts, where we lived. Waiting in the chilly parking lot for my father to pick up my mother and me—my brother, two years my junior, had been deemed too young for the movie—I realized that I had been permitted to go to an over three-hour movie on a school night because this was not an entertainment but an event, an event that was significant in the life of the small but intense Jewish community of which we were a part. The nature of this significance was perfectly clear to all of us. *Judgment at Nuremberg* was the first time in general American mass culture in which the terrible things that had been done to the Jews of Europe were being publicly acknowledged. Although it was not talked about very openly, the murder of European Jewry was a tragedy we were all aware of, and by "we" I mean teenagers like myself as well as grown-ups. But as Jews, we regarded this knowledge as a private sorrow that was not shared by the non-Jewish majority of Americans. This new motion picture, straight from Hollywood with a panoply of stars, changed that. So that despite whatever Stanley Kramer was saying in his interviews in the *New York Times* and elsewhere, we had our own conviction of what *Judgment at Nuremberg* was "about." It was about the Holocaust, although we would not have used that term because it was not yet current.

I am astonished to think that this is what we thought as I return to the movie thirty-five years later in an era saturated with Holocaust studies and Holocaust consciousness. For if this is a motion picture about the destruction of European Jewry, then where are the Jews? You can scrutinize the film from reel to reel and find no Jews whatsoever. Yes, the prosecutor does mention in passing that six million Jews were killed, but this is after he has introduced the concentration camp footage by saying that the victims came from every country in occupied Europe. The Jews are mentioned among others, and that is the solitary reference. Unlike the Eichmann trial, in which many Jewish survivors were called as witnesses, no Jews are called to testify in the courtroom depicted in *Judgment at Nuremberg*. The only representation of a Jew in the film is the lecherous image of the older man with whom Irene Hoffman was unjustly supposed to have had relations. This effacement of the Jewish identity of the victims, moreover, remained completely unremarked upon in the critical notices of the film in its time. Entirely characteristic is the indefinite universality—and the lack of interest in historical fact—of the review in *Variety* when it speaks of "a period in which 6,000,000 innocent persons were murdered."[31] It was not until much later, in the writings of Lawrence Langer, Judith Doneson, and Ilan Avisar, that the disappearance of the Jews in the film was clearly registered; and this delay in marking a fact that now seems so self-evident is another reminder of the enormous shift that took place in our perception of the Holocaust.[32]

So, in retrospect, it seems to me that we were wrong and Kramer was wrong, but in unequal measures. Though exaggerated, Kramer's claim that, despite its ostensible subject, his film is "really" about the American national character has some foundation in film; there are allusions and references that make the American theme palpable if not primary. Yet the efforts of contemporary American Jewish viewers to recoup the film as a statement about the Jewish Holocaust strike us now as a projection onto the film of a deeply held desire for wider American acknowledgment of a Jewish catastrophe that they themselves had only recently come to admit more fully. This projection was far from naive. American Jews, I think, assumed that there were many subjects that the Hollywood studios simply would not put on the big screen. That the fact of the Holocaust was presented in *Judgment at Nuremberg* and documentary footage shown was taken as a source of wonderment; that the Holocaust as a "parochial" tragedy for the Jewish people should be represented was considered beyond all expectation. Jewish viewers therefore saw themselves as receptors of an encoded communication; they picked up and discreetly unscrambled signals of what could not be said.

And yet. Although the makers and sponsors of the film wanted

The Holocaust at the Movies

only to invoke the specter of the Holocaust in order to focus on the question of guilt and responsibility, they could not exert complete control over the forces they had summoned up. There are elements in *Judgment at Nuremberg* that resemble unstable, radioactive compounds that, though shielded and stoppered, produce unpredicted effects. The concentration camp footage is the most obvious of these, but not the only one. Unsupported by historical argument and explanation, the footage is used for its immediate, visceral impact on the viewer and then put aside. But the genie cannot so quickly be put back in the bottle. The aura of the images fades but does not disappear. There occurs a kind of representational seepage that continues to lay down its own film of consciousness independent of its celluloid embodiment. The scope of what is representable in this medium has been enlarged. Something has changed.

Unintended, too, are the effects of the Nazi songs and Volkish culture that Kramer uses in the picture to give us an authentic taste of time and place. This long movie begins and ends with an identical long sequence in which we see the unmoving logo of the seven stars in profile on the screen while we listen to military marches sung in German by an unseen all-male chorus. Sung with full-throated gusto, these rousing songs are presumably ones that accompanied the goose-stepping storm troopers as they marched at the great Nazi rallies. Sure enough, this is the same kind of music we hear when, upon arriving in the city, Spencer Tracy visits the stadium where the Nuremberg rallies were held and imagines what must have gone on there. Meant simply to provide a historical frame of reference, these abandoned and exhilarating marches break free of their intended purpose. They fascinate and arouse us and, in so doing, spill over into the problematic domain of Nazi kitsch that Saul Freidlander has described so well.[33] Similarly, there is the scene of communal singing in the beer hall Spencer Tracy visits with Marlene Dietrich immediately after the shocking films have been shown in the courtroom. Bosley Crowther, writing in the *New York Times*, sees in all this nostalgic good cheer, singing of sentimental love songs, and bang-

In his performance as the defense counsel, Maximillian Schell displays a mercurial and brilliant brooding that contrasts with Richard Widmark's plodding and strident performance as the American Prosecutor. *Judgment at Nuremberg.*

ing of beer steins an "old-fashioned *gemuetlichkeit*" that he thinks is obviously "created for the benefit of the audience which is thus made to feel a warm compassion for the people of Germany" as a counterbalance to the acts carried out by some others of the German people.[34] This may indeed be what the director intended as well, yet the jarring juxtaposition between the scenes of atrocity and the transported singing, in which individual sorrows are dissolved into collective exaltation, can lead to quite other associations.

Finally, there is the mercurial charisma of Maximilian Schell. Perhaps the least known and the least expensive of the Fabulous Seven, he was nevertheless the only one from the cast of the Playhouse Ninety television production to have been retained for the film ver-

The Holocaust at the Movies

sion of *Judgment at Nuremberg*. Compared to his opposite number—Richard Widmark's strident, monotonous, and crude portrayal of the army prosecutor—Schell is subtle, brilliant, resourceful, and winning as the young defense counsel. In the dramatic economy of the production, his true antagonist is Spencer Tracy himself. As the plain-spoken and incorruptible American judge, Tracy's understated performance embodies the stolid weight and authority of American decency. Yet Schell's thrusts of rhetorical eloquence, his passionate and unapologetic patriotism, and his shrewd use of American jurisprudence in his arguments (Justice Holmes's condoning of forced sterilization, for example) make him a center of energy that has no like in the film. His message, that the defendants in the dock were not the source of Germany's problems and that to find them guilty would be counterproductive to Germany's recovery as a healthy and democratic nation, is decisively refuted. But the charisma of his presence ultimately steals the show. It is an unwitting theft with unforeseen consequences.

THE PAWNBROKER (1965)

In his 1988 study *Screening the Holocaust*, the Israeli-born critic Ilan Avisar explains why he finds Sidney Lumet's 1965 film, *The Pawnbroker*, so offensive. He finds the analogy established in the picture between street violence in American cities and the murder of European Jewry in concentration camps to be bogus and disturbing. Further insult is added by the portrayal of Jews vis-à-vis blacks and Puerto Ricans. Jesús Ortiz, the pawnbroker's assistant, his girlfriend, and mother are all presented as sympathetic victims who are full of vitality, aspiration, and domestic or passionate love. By contrast, the Jewish characters are mindless, self-pitying, greedy, materialistic, and grotesque. Sol Nazerman, the pawnbroker who ostensibly despises humanity and cares only for money, is made into a latter-day embodiment of the Jewish preoccupation with mercantile success. "Thus," writes Avisar, "the anguish of Jewish history is used insidiously to strengthen one of the most negative stereotypes of Jews as heartless money-makers." The final offense is provided by the overlay of Christianity. When Jesús Ortiz steps in front of Nazerman during a holdup and takes the bullet meant for the pawnbroker, he renders, Christlike, the ultimate sacrifice, and this has the effect of melting the Jew's hardness of heart. Nazerman "is literally Christianized through love, grace, and suffering."[35]

I too find myself offended, and with many of the same grievances as Avisar. Yet I feel more intrigued than outraged. Looking back over the responses to the film when it appeared in 1965, I am surprised that not more offense was taken. Moreover, it is just those assumptions about eternal Jewish suffering and Christian love—the core of the insult—that were taken for granted by most viewers at the time as natural and appropriate to the movie's theme. My conclusion is that Ilan Avisar and I, while admittedly speaking from a stance within Jewish culture, belong chronologically to a kind of second phase of consciousness about the Holocaust that evolved in the seventies and eighties. Looking backward from the other side of this imaginary dividing line, the cultural products of an earlier time, and *The Pawnbroker* among them, look very different now than they once did.

Understanding the nature of that difference is doubly important now that the Holocaust has inscribed itself at the center of our public discourse. Looking back at films like *Judgment at Nuremberg* and *The Pawnbroker*, which were breakthrough films in their time, makes us aware of two critical points: how relatively recent is our "Holocaust consciousness" and how particularly American were the terms on which the Holocaust purchased its foothold in our culture.

Those American terms, moreover, were far from static. Just how quickly the cultural ground was shifting in the sixties is evident in the differences between these two films, one made in 1961 and the other in 1965. In *Judgment at Nuremberg*, the earlier film, the idea of American justice, though threatened from many sides, not only perseveres but prevails. The Germans may evade responsibility for

The Holocaust at the Movies

heinous wartime crimes, and American politicians and military commanders may counsel expediency, but there exists a plainspoken American judge who knows the difference between right and wrong and will not betray that trust. It is with his perspective that we are invited to identify, and that norm remains viable if embattled. Just four years later, however, *The Pawnbroker* unfolds a picture of American urban life so submerged in oppression that only a comparison to the Nazi concentration camps can suggest its true depths. From such suffering there can be no way out and no collective solution, only exceptional acts of empathy that fellow sufferers can offer one another. The evil resides, moreover, not abroad but at home; and it is this bitter cavalcade of victimization that becomes the most essential definition of America at mid-century.

Thus, despite their proximity in time, one film reflects backward while the other film reflects the ferment of social change in the present. *Judgment at Nuremberg* does register anxieties about the excesses of the Cold War and the legacy of racial bigotry—recall the black Marine sentry's reaction when he heard about the hanging of children—but its heart is set on rallying support for the foundational values of fairness and equality that had given meaning to our defeat of fascism and justification to the era of prosperity and national celebration that followed the war. *The Pawnbroker*, on the other hand, gives expression to a new mood of social conscience. "Social conscience" is a term from the parlance of the time, and I use it here to underscore a set of attitudes held by intellectuals toward the social turmoil of the 1960s. How these attitudes diffused into the mainstream of American culture through a Hollywood movie like *The Pawnbroker* and how the connection was made to the Holocaust are among the questions that concern us.

The civil rights movement, with its acts of nonviolent protest and its fiery martyrdoms, provided a touchstone to moral conscience such as was not seen in America since the days of abolitionism. For intellectuals on the Left, the civil rights movement in the South—and even northern inner-city violence—gave belated confirmation to a critique of American society that been current since the twenties and thirties in socialist circles, both communist and anticommunist. The new mood of conscience was much less ideological and much more populist. America came to be seen as a society compromised at its core by inequality and oppression, and this was a conception held by a broad spectrum of religious leaders, writers, and university students: in short, people of "conscience" generally.

The sense of responsibility for this suffering weighed heavily. Though less quietly than some others, white liberal intellectuals—the children of Jewish immigrants prominent among them—identified with this central moral failing of the American commonweal. "Few are guilty," goes one of the slogans of the time, "but all are responsible." Yet the new attitudes brought with them not just a conviction of culpability but also an opportunity for moral regeneration. The call to "social action" provided a way out of the malaise defined by American versions of postwar European existentialism. Through "sensitivity," an empathic connection to the suffering of the oppressed, and through "commitment," an active engagement in movements and demonstrations of protest, the individual might break free of the toils of anomie, inauthenticity, and alienation.

In Hollywood of mid-century there were few filmmakers who better embodied the ethos of social conscience than Sidney Lumet. Born in 1924, Lumet was the son of an actor in Maurice Schwartz's Yiddish Art Theatre and as a child appeared on the Yiddish stage on New York's Lower East Side. As a young man he moved on to the world of Broadway theater and acted in dramas that dealt with social class and ethnic problems, such as *Brooklyn, U.S.A.* and *One Third of the Nation*. Lumet directed hundreds of programs during the heyday of serious drama on television in the fifties; many of these took up themes of individual responsibility for social ills and were presented—to the degree permitted by the medium—through the lens of urban realism. *Twelve Angry Men* (1957), Lumet's first feature film, is the story of a lone juror who must convince eleven others of a young Puerto Rican man's innocence; it has been read as a

The Holocaust at the Movies

"rebuttal to the lynch-mob hysteria of the McCarthy era" and as an "anti-conformist tract and a plea for legitimate justice and civil rights."[36] Lumet went on to a prolific career as a movie director who specialized in film adaptations of serious plays (by playwrights such as Tennessee Williams, Eugene O'Neill, Arthur Miller) and in gritty police dramas centering on issues of guilt and responsibility and set in the multiethnic turmoil of New York City (*Serpico, Prince of the City, Q & A*). His controversial adaptation of E. M. Doctorow's *The Book of Daniel* (1980) revisited and revised memories of the Old Left and the Rosenberg executions. Even though Lumet's output has been enormous and varied, one of the chief characteristics of his work remains a concern for social justice and individual responsibility.

Lumet's work in film can usefully be seen as a point of cultural transfer between the attitudes of the liberal classes in America and those of a larger popular audience. This is not to say that he was a fellow traveler who used the media to propagate specific ideological values; Lumet was his own man, who preferred to base his films on imaginative works of literature rather than on political tracts. Yet his films do reflect an outlook on humanity and society that can be located on the politic map of the times. So the question remains why a director with Lumet's concerns should want to make a film in which the Holocaust figures prominently. There were many other figures in Hollywood with Jewish backgrounds who evinced no interest in the subject, which, moreover, on commercial grounds, held little allure for American viewers. Why then should Lumet be interested in the Holocaust?

We can begin to answer the question by underscoring an obvious fact about *The Pawnbroker*. The movie is not about the Holocaust as a whole but about the life of a survivor. In contrast to *Judgment at Nuremberg*, there is little interest in Lumet's film in the motives of the perpetrators and the historical conditions in which the event took place. Like the claustrophobic cage of Nazerman's pawnshop, the film's narrow focus is trained on its essential innovation: the damaged inner life of a Holocaust survivor. The film focuses, moreover, on the present configuration of that damage. The causes of the damage are supplied by the flashbacks of Nazerman's experience in the concentration camps. The film, however, is ultimately interested less in etiology than in pathology. It seeks to present a character study in the present that maps the deformations of Nazerman's self.

In diagnosing Nazerman's condition, contemporary comment stressed his detachment from his fellow human beings as the pathological outcome of his suffering. Nazerman's wartime experiences have made him settle for "a wholly mercenary, unfeeling life as a pawnbroker in New York's Spanish Harlem," which he devotes to the business of dispossessing the downtrodden of the last tokens of their dreams. "For him, all people now are 'scum.'"[37] "He stands armored in unfeelingness," writes Brendan Gill in the New Yorker, "and one sees by every sagging muscle of his fat, middle-aged body as it shuffles about the shop and by the shallow singsong of his tired voice as he deals with one or another of his troubled customers that he has made himself inhumanly safe—safe even from the threat of death, which he would not lift a finger to delay."[38] He is a man who, as Bosley Crowther writes in the New York Times, "has reasonably eschewed a role of involvement and compassion in a brutal world and has found his life barren and footless as a consequence." His life is marked by a profound "detachment and inability to adjust."[39]

It is Nazerman's debased detachment that is overcome in the course of the action. A "shattering excess of mental torment" and the self-sacrifice of his young Puerto Rican assistant finally break down the pawnbroker's estrangement and jolt him into an acknowledgment of the "shame of his detachment" and "his burden of grief and guilt." For Crowther, The Pawnbroker is a "drama of discovery of the need of man to try to do something for his fellow human sufferers in the troubled world of today."[40] Similarly, for Brendan Gill the movie tells the story of how the pawnbroker's "armor is stripped off and poor Nazerman is restored, naked and suffering, to

The Holocaust at the Movies

His heart hardened by his losses and suffering, the pawnbroker, Sol Nazerman (Rod Steiger), dispossesses his customers of their last illusions. *The Pawnbroker,* Allied Artists

the hell of the living."[41] Nazerman's "regeneration," then, involves not the alleviation of his suffering but a new and more acute capacity to feel pain, the pain of others as well as his own crushing memories. Rather than being shut up in a prison of cynicism and contempt, Nazerman now reenters life by joining the world of fellow sufferers.

The emphasis on Nazerman as a monster of detachment moves us closer to explaining this first appearance of a Holocaust survivor as the hero of a Hollywood feature film. Detachment is understood in *The Pawnbroker* as a process in which, because of unspeakable suffering, a person severs connections to others, becomes insensible to their pain, and thereby withdraws from the interconnectedness of humanity. Within the ethos of social conscience, detachment is the ultimate sin; it is the antithesis of sensitivity and makes engagement and commitment impossible. Two things are crucial in the portrayal of Nazerman: the degree of his suffering and the fact that there are reasons for it. His moral disfigurement is extreme because his victimization has been extreme. It is not the vagaries of temperament and human nature that have made Nazerman callous and offensive but historical persecutions more hideous than can be imagined. The survivor thus becomes an extreme case of an endemic social ailment: the moral disfigurement that results from oppression. The Jew in this deformed state ironically becomes a luminous standard by which the suffering of others can be understood and their depravity revealed as the inevitable outcome of persecution.

Yet despite its status as an exemplum of misery born of "man's inhumanity to man," the figure of Nazerman in *The Pawnbroker* does not lose its particularity. The nearly total effacement of the Jews in *Judgment at Nuremberg* and its critical reception reflected an earlier era in which, in the mind of the media, the Jews were folded into the generality of victims of Nazism, and in which the Jews themselves did not seek to call attention to the distinctiveness of their victimization. In *The Pawnbroker*, in contrast, Nazerman's Jewishness is of the essence, and there is no confusion about the Jewishness of the concentration camp inmates who appear in the flashbacks. The specificity of the portrait of the survivor is reinforced by the idiosyncratic collection of mannerisms gathered around the character of Nazerman in Rod Steiger's performance, which was regarded by many viewers as a stunning piece of virtuosity.[42] Nazerman's inner life, which is perceived as impenetrable and unfeeling by his humiliated customers, the denizens of Harlem who surround him, is revealed to us in the classic mode of dramatic irony. The flashes of memory that crack open Nazerman's unyielding facade cannot be seen by the blacks and Puerto Ricans with whom he comes in daily contact and who therefore can have no comprehension of the causes of his meanness. It is only we the viewers who are given the possibility of empathy by possessing this knowledge, which, though privileged, remains ineffectual in mitigating the tragic denouement.

The flashbacks, which provide a fragmentary imbedded narrative concerning the degradation and murder of Nazerman's family and friends in the camps, were one of the most celebrated features of the film.[43] The deployment of this technique raised Lumet in the minds of some to the status of not just a film director but an auteur. Lumet uses flashback "to stunning effect in *The Pawnbroker*," asserts Philip T. Hartung in *Commonweal*, "flashbacks that are as startling in their past-is-present implications as those in *Wild Strawberries* and *Hiroshima, Mon Amour*."[44] The flashbacks are indeed Lumet's contribution if not his invention. In the novel by Edward Lewis Wallant, upon which the movie is based, these incursions of the past appear as dreams, and they are printed in italics to distinguish them from Nazerman's waking consciousness. In making the dreams into flashbacks, Lumet was able not only to fashion a cinematographic equivalent to the dreams but also to push the point further by making these eruptions disturb Nazerman's waking rather than sleeping mental state.[45]

Coming several years after Wiesel's *Night*, Lumet's *The Pawnbroker* had a significant influence in shaping the image of the survivor in American culture. Although it will not be until later that the survivor attains the status of a cultural hero, we now see the figure emerging from the underground and establishing itself as a representative and therefore legitimate American type. The survivor is a type, moreover, that has its own claims to make; it embodies a grim authenticity and bears witness to an undeniable dimension of modern Jewish experience. Yet it is important to be precise concerning what the survivor is supposed to be *about* in this early stage of the image's development. *The Pawnbroker* supports the notion of the survivor's self as construed entirely under the sign of rupture. The Nazerman we see in the opening slow-motion flashback—a vigorous, smiling man secure in the lap of nature and in the love of his children, wife, and parents, and a professor of philosophy, to boot—is utterly discontinuous with the craven misanthrope who plies the trade of dispossession among the already dispossessed. If there is any continuity it is only the residue of erudition with which Nazerman expresses contempt for his customers.

That the survivor should naturally be a broken man and a morally disfigured man is respectfully acknowledged by contemporary reviewers. Writing about the film in the Zionist journal *Midstream*, Albert Bermel credits Lumet, following Wallant's novel, with having done his research into the "psychopathology of Nazerman" and having documented what psychiatry had begun to call "the concentration camp syndrome or the survivor syndrome." Quoting from contemporary accounts, Bermel describes the syndrome as characterized by "morose behavior, withdrawal, general apathy alternating with occasional short-lived angry outbursts, . . . pervasive guilt, . . . and spells of confusion with the past—when every building looks to them like the Auschwitz blockhouse, every policeman like an S.S. guard."[46] What Bermel finds fault with in the movie is not the clinical accuracy of the portrait but Lumet's failure to find the artistic means to make the syndrome convincing and his reliance instead on frenzy and hysteria.

In the major contemporary responses to *The Pawnbroker*, I have found only one voice, that of Stanley Kauffmann in *The New Republic*, that does not take for granted the conception of the survivor as broken. For Kauffmann, Sol Nazerman's behavior is not self-evident and requires an explanation that the film never supplies.

> Why is Sol still so much in the grip of the past? Why is this particular survivor so specially paralyzed? Many of us have known people who have suffered similarly, suffered so grossly that the fact of life thereafter seems (to us) incredible; yet there they are living—working, quarreling, remarrying, propagating deliberately (in one case I know) to refute the ovens. They are certainly not unmarked or forgetful; yet they are certainly not numb like Sol. I do not argue that all people must respond similarly to experience, only that because Sol is such a remarkable exception, we miss an explanation.[47]

The Holocaust at the Movies

For his sense of the norm to which Nazerman is a remarkable exception, Kauffmann draws not on literature and cinema but on his anecdotal experience of the world around him. Kauffmann's minority opinion helps us to identify an interesting and ironic moment of divergence in the mid-sixties between two conceptions of the survivor. The one stresses the sterile dysfunctionality, and even depravity, of the survivor, while the other stresses the generative and energetic, even aggressive, adaptation to renewed life. Although all survivors are plagued by nightmares and guilt in this second conception, those who are truly paralyzed represent an extreme of "psychopathology" that does not comport with the evidence of day-to-day life. It is in such powerful works of the imagination as *Night* and *The Pawnbroker* that the first conception is amplified, and, at least for the critical community at this point in time, it is the pathological model that proves most persuasive.

The reasons for this preference may be rooted in the film's dour vision of Jewish history as a whole. It may sound grandiose to speak of the film's possessing such a vision, but Lumet, following Wallant, aspires to do more than give us a study of a Holocaust survivor. There is, to be sure, the sharply rendered picture of Sol Nazerman, whose mannered specificity is matched by the grittily observed urban scenes around him. But there is also an allegorical level on which the pawnbroker comes to stand for nothing less than the travails of the Jewish people throughout history. That larger meaning is easily enough stated: because of their exile and persecution, the Jews have hardened themselves to human feeling and turned their energy to business. Take, for example, Nazerman's discourse about the Jews, which he delivers to Jesús Ortiz in response to the assistant's repeated pleas to reveal the secrets of the Jews' success in business.

> You begin with several thousand years during which you have nothing except a great, bearded legend, nothing else. You have no land to grow food on, no land on which to hunt, not enough time in one place to have a geography or an army or a land-myth. Only you

have a little brain in your head and this bearded legend to sustain you and convince you that there *is* something special about you, even in your poverty. But this little brain, that is the real key. With it you obtain a small piece of cloth—wool, silk, cotton—it doesn't matter. You take this cloth and you cut it in two and sell the two pieces for a penny or two more than you paid for the one. With this money, then, you buy a slightly larger piece of cloth, which perhaps may be cut into three pieces and sold for *three* pennies' profit. You must never succumb to buying an extra piece of bread at this point, a luxury like a toy for your child. Immediately you must go out and buy a still-larger cloth, or two large cloths, and repeat the process. And so you continue until there is no longer any temptation to dig in the earth and grow food, no longer any desire to gaze at limitless land which is in your name. You repeat this process over and over and over for approximately twenty centuries. And then, *voila*—you have a mercantile heritage, you are known as a merchant, a man with secret resources, usurer, pawnbroker, witch, and what have you.[48]

Rod Steiger's delivery of this speech is a tour de force of bitter mockery; Jesús has respectfully requested some advice on how to succeed in business, and what he gets flung at him is a philosophy of history.

Yet beneath the barbed hyperbole is a serious message whose intellectual provenance is remarkably diverse: Elizabethan stereotypes, nineteenth-century anti-Semitism, Marxist theory, and even Zionist ideology. Undergirding the ideas expressed in the speech, I see, in general terms, a version of the classic liberal-Enlightenment analysis of Jews. In their present state, such an analysis argues, the Jews are an ugly people, unfeeling, morally obtuse, and obsessed with money to the exclusion of all higher sentiments. Yet their preoccupation with business, and their expertise at it, are in fact adaptive strategies that evolved long ago as a compensation for being dispossessed of a land of their own and the morally healthy life that could have been lived upon it. Sustained by a religious mystification (the

The Holocaust at the Movies

"bearded legend"), the Jews have denied themselves pleasure and compassion in order to survive in a hostile world.

In this long view of Jewish experience, the destruction of European Jewry is not a shattering rupture but a consummation. The Holocaust serves as a supercharged symbol of the sorry persecution and degradation of the Jews over the centuries; and the survivor therefore becomes not an idiosyncratic marginal type but an exemplar of his people's fortunes. Compared with the only other Jews in the film—Nazerman's sister's family, with whom he lives in a Long Island tract house—the survivor is in fact a paragon of authenticity. His suffering has been painfully real and the concomitant moral disfigurement enormous. In their grasping materialism and superficiality, Nazerman's American Jewish relatives are not vastly superior to him, yet they have no suffering or persecution with which to justify their turpitude.

The notion of the Holocaust survivor as The Jew served a curious apologetic purpose for Lumet and the bearers of social conscience of the time. It enabled them to condemn the American Jewish reality as they saw it—the chauvinistic, self-absorbed, frivolous march of the children of Jewish immigrants into the middle classes—while at the same time absolving themselves of the charge of self-hatred. For they knew that this success-obsessed betrayal of sensitivity and social values was not the essential historical character of the Jews but a response to a chain of persecutions of which the Holocaust was the most searing, the most palpable, and the most sensational.

The receptivity to the notion of the survivor as the Eternal Jew, it should be noted, was strong even within enlightened Jewish circles at the time of the film's release. In *Midstream: A Quarterly Jewish Review*, published by the Theodore Herzl Foundation, Albert Bermel's intelligent comparison between the Wallant novel and the Lumet film opens with the observation that

> The theme of the late Edward Lewis Wallant's novel *The Pawnbroker* is the eternal sufferings of the Jew brought to a humiliating climax

in our time. In adapting the book to the film, Sidney Lumet, the director, has tried to intensify the sufferings, coaxing them on, as it were, employing the resources of cinema to construct an interplay of the sufferings that well up from within and the sufferings imposed from without.[49]

The problem Bermel addresses in his lengthy assessment of the picture is essentially an aesthetic one: Lumet's artless reliance on frenzy and hysteria rather than emotional argument and motivation. The means do not support the message, he is saying, but the worthiness of the message itself is taken for granted.

> [Lumet's] social conscience is irreproachable; his aims are admirable; his art is negligible. To make of Nazerman the Eternal Jew and to make his sufferings cry out for the sufferings of all Jewry he would have had to show damage farther-reaching than blood and physical hurts.[50]

However ill served by the film, the message remains an irreproachable expression of social conscience. This is precisely the message that proved so offensive a generation later to a critic such as Ilan Avisar, who, in commenting on Nazerman's speech to Ortiz on the development of the "mercantile heritage" among the Jews, has this to say: "Thus the anguish of Jewish history is used insidiously to strengthen one of the most negative stereotypes of Jews as heartless money-makers."[51]

What rankled most for latter-day viewers of *The Pawnbroker* was the contrast between a Christian ethos of love and the degraded state of the Jews. Through its unremitting crosscutting approach, the film sets up a programmatic series of juxtapositions between the conduct and family relations of Jesús Ortiz and those of Sol Nazerman. Repentant of his past criminality, Ortiz is determined to work hard and make an honest life for himself; he has hope for his own future and sees the inherent dignity in poor souls that fre-

The Holocaust at the Movies

The Jewish pawnbroker accedes to the request of his Puerto Rican assistant, Jesús (Jaime Sanchez), to teach him the secrets of gold. *The Pawnbroker*

quent the pawnshop. These are the same creatures Nazerman views as scum, for he is beyond hope and has hardened his heart to all human feeling. The relations between Ortiz and his mother are awash in tenderness and mutual respect, whereas Nazerman despises his sister's family, whose members suck up to him because he supports them. The camera mercilessly cuts between scenes of Ortiz's relations with his girlfriend, Mabel, and Nazerman's relations with Tessie, the widow of a friend murdered in the camps. Ortiz and Mabel's lovemaking is full of pleasure and affection, and Mabel, though a prostitute, encourages Ortiz's honest ambitions and seeks to join him in his hopeful vision of the future. Nazerman and Tessie's weekly gropings are desultory and pleasureless and are conducted under a barrage of curses from Tessie's dying father in the next room.

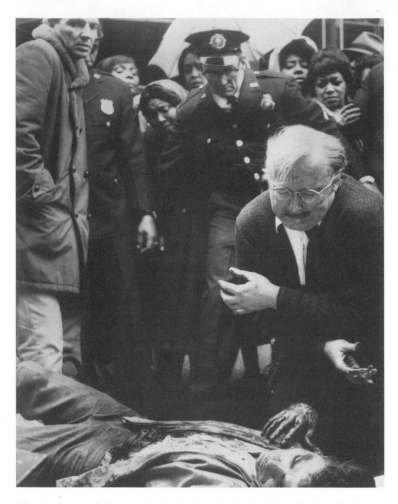

The hardness of the pawnbroker's heart is finally pierced when Jesús sacrifices his life for him. *The Pawnbroker*

The Holocaust at the Movies

But that is not all. Just as Nazerman is not only an individual pawn-broker who is a Holocaust survivor but also the Eternal Jew, so too does Jesús Ortiz take on aspects of his Christian name. He is tempted and almost falls—driven to temptation by the Jew's rejection of his discipleship—and visits a church before finally sacrificing himself for the protection and redemption of his Jewish master. Whether the portals of the pawnbroker's heart are indeed opened by this ulti-mate gesture of love remains equivocal. Nazerman cradles Ortiz in the Pieta position and lets out a great soundless cry of anguish, his first overt expression of grief. In Wallant's novel, Nazerman recon-nects with this family by calling his nephew Morton and asking him to come into the shop the next day to help him, and then, connected in grief to all he has lost—including Ortiz—he heads downtown "to take the long underground journey to Tessie's house, to help her mourn."[52] In Lumet's film version, however, Nazerman reenters the pawnshop and impales his hands on a spike punch used for customer receipts; with blood dripping from these stigmata he wanders out among the urban crowd, alone and directionless. There are no stig-mata in the novel, and, as Bermel and others have pointed out, the insertion of this scene is consistent with Lumet's intervention throughout the film to deepen Nazerman's isolation as well as his resistance to even the adumbrations of salvation.

For a critic like Avisar, the recourse to Christology is the great-est insult, all the more so because someone like Sidney Lumet, who grew up in the lap of the Yiddish theater in New York's Lower East Side, should know better. Yet for contemporary reviewers, finding references to Christ in works of modern art about great suffering was a most natural occurrence, as was the search for hints of alle-gory in general. Bosley Crowther in the *New York Times* opens his review with what he takes as the key to the movie's intention. Steiger's character "casts, as it were, the somber shadow of the legendary, age-less Wandering Jew. That is the mythical Judean who taunted Jesus on the way to Calvary and was condemned to roam the world a lonely outcast until Jesus should come again."[53]

The Holocaust at the Movies

For Louis Chapin in the *Christian Science Monitor*, "The answer to the Jew's hopeless bewilderment is spelled out when through an impulse of Christian sacrifice his life is saved by his apprentice."[54] These viewers, apparently like Lumet himself, saw nothing provocative or outrageous in mixing and matching Jewish Holocaust survivors with Christian motifs. It was the general perception at the time in liberal artistic circles—and not there alone, of course—that the *metier* of the Jews was suffering and downtroddenness, but when it came to salvation and the transfiguring passion of suffering, this was the proper sphere of Christianity. It was here one looked for gestures of selflessness, sacrifice, and regeneration.

Yet in the end, the Christian symbolism turns out to be nothing less than an irksome distraction from the real conceptual nub of the film: the analogy between Harlem and the Holocaust, between ghetto and ghetto, between urban violence in America and Nazi brutality. In her 1983 study, *Indelible Shadows,* Annette Insdorf puts it in this way:

> While it is admittedly a facile distortion to posit a one-to-one analogy between the Harlem ghetto in 1965 and the camps of the early forties, Nazerman treats his predominantly black customers with the same disdain that characterized the Nazis' attitude toward Jews. He calls them "creatures," "scum," "rejects"—and his job is ultimately one of dispossession. Indeed, the pawnbroker can be seen as a contemporary Kapo, controlling the poor clients who barter with him, but also controlled—and imprisoned—by his superiors.[55]

While the analogy may indeed be facile and while Lumet may have denied positing it,[56] there is no avoiding the fact that, as Avisar asserts, "his film projects exactly that notion."[57] The flashbacks are the major device that establishes the analogy; instances of violence (Nazerman witnessing a man being beaten up) or depravation (the pregnant girl's engagement ring) trigger memories of the horrors of the camps in a way that makes the comparison unavoidable. The comparison is

The Holocaust at the Movies

maintained in a more subtle way by Boris Kaufman's cinematography, which unrelievedly shoots Steiger from behind the grates and bars on the pawnshop in which he is imprisoned.

Is the comparison bogus or illuminating? The objections stem from both sides of the equation. From the earlier vantage point of a film like *Judgment at Nuremberg* and the complex of attitudes it represents, what is intolerable is the belittlement of American justice that comes from comparing American social reality to conditions under the Nazis. For students of European Jewry a generation later, what is intolerable is the belittlement of the Holocaust that comes from comparing it to social ills, however degrading and demoralizing, that take place in a society that has provisions for dissent and legal process. For Lumet, the trajectory of the analogy is clear. He treats the murder of European Jewry and its traumatic effects on survivors with the utmost seriousness, and he has given us the first persuasive representation in cinema of the inner world of the survivor. Yet at the same time, Lumet uses the Holocaust for an ulterior purpose: to leverage concern for the tragedy of the urban ghettos and the ordeal of the American underclass. The Holocaust serves as a frame of reference of unspeakable horror, and it is by connecting the plight of the urban poor to this ultimate, extraterritorial standard that the catastrophe here at home can be rendered palpable for American men and women of social conscience.

SCHINDLER'S LIST (1993)

Although the two films we have discussed so far are important landmarks in the reception of the Holocaust in America, the impact of *Schindler's List* is an event of an entirely different order of magnitude. The only true comparison is outside of film altogether: the 1978 television miniseries *Holocaust*. Both productions were seen by an extraordinary number of Americans (over 120 million); both productions were accompanied by vast educational campaigns; and both were the trigger for creating new institutions for memorializing the Holocaust. In both cases, moreover, the critical reception was deeply divided, and along similar lines. Ordinary viewers, the popular media, and communal organizations saw in both the miniseries and the film a momentous breakthrough. Despite their flaws, these works were held to be capable of imparting an awareness of the Holocaust to millions of people who would otherwise remain ignorant of the event; and they were further credited with success in "moving" people, that is making the imparted knowledge affecting, in ways in that more austere works of art had failed to do. The detractors were intellectuals and academics who argued that both *Holocaust* and *Schindler's List* had absorbed the catastrophe into the sentimental and melodramatic conventions of popular entertainment and in so doing had betrayed the event, even if they had spread its impact more broadly.[58]

Now, the differences between the television series and the movie are admittedly significant, and not just because of the separate character of each medium and the divergent conception of each project. In terms of sheer artistry and technical brilliance, most viewers placed *Schindler's List* in a class by itself. Spielberg himself, with his history of stunning box-office successes, was an overwhelming presence in a way in which the producers and directors of *Holocaust* were not.[59] The fifteen years that intervened between the two projects, moreover, had created a different climate for works about the Holocaust. Nonetheless, after taking all these evident differences into account, the similarities of the debate remain striking: the identity of the parties to the debate, the depth of the cleavage, and the ferocity of the discussion.

In the case of *Schindler's List* especially, the volume of response has been enormous, and there has been an appreciable increase in the amount of academic reflection on the work, in keeping with the film's greater artistic ambitions and the general growth of professional attention to the Holocaust in the academy. To find a way through this wealth of material I propose the following itinerary: first, to understand the substance of the arguments put forward on behalf of the film; second, to probe the substance of the offense taken by the film's critics; and finally to explore the characteristically American nature of the terms underlying both sides of the debate.

The Case For Schindler's List

Most critics who ended by praising *Schindler's List* first approached the film with dread. "I . . . was afraid of seeing terrible events sentimentalized," writes John Gross in the *New York Review of Books*, "afraid of sentimentality proving all the more insidious for being applied with sleek technical skill."[60] Although Spielberg had applied himself—with mixed success—to two films with serious themes (*The Color Purple* and *Empire of the Sun*), his fame rested on movies of adventure and fantasy that deployed an ambitious arsenal of cutting-edge special effects. The only Nazis who had appeared in his films were the fun-and-games kind in his Indiana Jones trilogy. The idea that this director would apply his particular craft to the realities of mass killings and death camps provoked the prospect of kitsch at best and sacrilege at worst. It is therefore an astonishing surprise and a great relief for a critic like Gross, whose taste is respected on both sides of the Atlantic, to report that the worst of his fears were "altogether mistaken." Spielberg's technical skills are in evidence, to be sure, but he "also shows a firm moral and emotional grasp of his material. The film is an outstanding achievement." Whereas the "filmmaking might have been Spielberg-clever," avers Stanley Kauffmann in *The New Republic*, it turns out that all "cleverness was renounced."[61]

What is at stake, in this view, is nothing less than the renunciation of artifice. The most successful filmmaker in the history of cinema is summoned by the pathos of the Holocaust to give up the bag of tricks he has used to cast a magic spell upon millions. Writes Julie Salamon in the *Wall Street Journal*: "This goes beyond his abandonment of techi tools: the Steadicam, the cranes, the zooming dolly shots. He has also abandoned the calculation one senses in many of his films, the shrewd commercial instinct for the note that will sell well, even though it may be tinny."[62] In place of artifice, Spielberg offers what Gross calls a "straightforward piece of storytelling." "The master showman grabbing at the lapels of exaltations," argues David Danby in *New York Magazine*, "has radically purified his methods," and he has produced an epic "in a style of austere realism—flat, angry, and hardheaded—that is utterly unlike anything Spielberg has attempted before."[63] Now, it is plain to all that a movie like *Schindler's List* could not be made without enormous sophistication; the very choice to film on black and white stock and to shoot on location in Poland are technical strategies aimed at enhancing the unadorned documentary effect. What the critics praise Spielberg for is his allowing himself be led and enlisted by the gravity of the event rather than relying upon his wizardlike capacity for manipulation.

Spielberg is also given high marks for the casting of the film and the shaping of the Schindler character. He resists the same temptation Stanley Kramer gave into in *Judgment at Nuremberg* to populate the film with well-known stars and recognized box-office draws. In deference to the seriousness of his subject, Spielberg used not-yet-famous actors for Schindler and Goeth, actors whose personae would not get in the way of the characters they were playing, or, in the case of Ben Kingsley, an actor with an uncanny talent for emptying his personality into his role. Across the board, Spielberg avoided American film actors, who would necessarily be embroiled in the world of Hollywood celebrity. For the hundreds of figures in the background of the film whose individual faces appear only briefly on the screen—including the *Schindlerjuden* themselves—Spielberg chose Polish and Israeli actors whose features are readily marked as East European. Spielberg's choices for the leading roles (there are really no secondary characters in the movie) and the performances they turn in are also judged to be extraordinary. Liam Neeson plays Oskar Schindler with "mesmerizing authority," says Janet Maslin, and Terrence Rafferty sees in Neeson's "quietly brilliant performance"

The Holocaust at the Movies

the "nuanced and utterly unsentimental acting" that is "exactly what the role requires."[64] Ralph Fiennes as Amon Goeth gets it right as well. He conveys Goeth's "sinister softness" and "touch of madness," according to John Gross, and he is particularly good "at bringing out the strong element of malevolent glee that so often accompanied Nazi atrocities."[65]

The epitome of Spielberg's newfound restraint is seen as his refusal to explain Oskar Schindler's conversion. Schindler begins the war as an opportunistic con man and entrepreneur whose employment of Jews recommends itself only because of its cheapness; he ends by using his wits and risking his life to save Jewish lives. A conventional narrative would feel constrained to offer explanatory perspectives on this enigma, but Spielberg desists, and his refusal is taken as a brilliant act of restraint. "Spielberg's artistic triumph here," writes Stanley Kauffmann, "is that he refuses to explicate, to interfere with what is actually known. He leaves the mystery of Schindler's goodness as finally inexplicable as the mystery of the 'human savagery' around him."[66] Terrence Rafferty goes so far as to propose a parallel between Schindler's moral conversion and the surprising course of Spielberg's own career.

> [H]eroism of this magnitude is, at its heart, inexplicable. Spielberg . . .
> also respects the mystery of Schindler's personality, and part of what
> makes the film so moving is that an ambiguous, complex hero is
> something entirely new in this director's work. The sheer unexpect-
> edness of Spielberg's rigorous refusal to simplify his protagonist's
> motives seems to connect him, in a minor but distinct way, to Schindler
> himself.[67]

A manipulator of audiences and a man of commercial transactions, Spielberg, like Schindler in darker times, has transcended himself by making this film, and this miracle, like the other, is better appreciated than dissected.

Acknowledged by many is the film's sheer power to move viewers, whether they be seasoned consumers of Holocaust information or the ill-informed and aloof. If *Schindler's List* had reached out to shake up its audience through atrocity and sensationalism, it would have taught nothing and left little impact, in addition to not having won the enormous viewership it did. But because Spielberg chose instead to make a film that is "[d]ark, sobering and also invigoratingly dramatic," Janet Maslin argues, "*Schindler's List* will make terrifying sense to anyone, anywhere."[68] The claim for the film's universal effectuality is tested not only in its impact on mass audiences but also, and perhaps more demandingly, in its ability to move even further those who feel they have been saturated with the subject and have already been moved as much as they would like to be. Take the case of David Denby, film critic for *New York Magazine*.

> *Schindler's List* left me shaken and not a little surprised. I didn't think I could be affected this way anymore, not by this subject. Like many people, I have gone through my share of Holocaust books and movies, and I thought I had learned most of what I had to learn. At the same time, I had become wary of Holocaust art as a temptation to emotional luxuriance and sadomasochistic titillation. Nor was I (or anyone else) willing to indulge a commercial entertainer eager to climb his way into Heaven through an exercise in penitential solemnity.[69]

Denby concludes that this "astounding achievement" results from the fact that, instead of jettisoning his instincts as an entertainer, Spielberg converted to a higher purpose the "same kinetic dynamism and weighted sense of movement he's always worked with."

Bringing a mass audience to tears over a historical catastrophe is a difficult end for a Hollywood film to achieve. Yet the real question is what is left after the image on the screen stops flickering and the emotion begins to fade. Here is the biggest compliment paid to *Schindler's List:* It has transcended its status as a movie and has become a monument. Just at a time when remembrance of the Holocaust was becoming institutionally established (the Washington museum had opened its doors eight months before the film's premier), reviewers express a widespread anxiety about the fading of the event within the collective memory of present and future generations. National polls showing increasing ignorance of the Holocaust among Americans are pointed to, as is the passing of the survivors, whose testimony is the last living link to the tragedy. As a bulwark against this tide stands *Schindler's List*. "As a contribution to popular culture, it can only do good," avers John Gross in the *New York Review of Books*. "Holocaust denial may or may not be a major problem in the future, but Holocaust ignorance, Holocaust forgetfulness, and Holocaust indifference are bound to be, and *Schindler's List* is likely to do as much as any single work can to dispel them."[70] For Janet Maslin, comparing *Schindler's List* to the billion-dollar grossing *Jurassic Park*, the film is destined to earn something better: "a permanent place in memory."[71] For Steven G. Kellman in *Midstream*, the film "will remain as our Homeric rendition of the Holocaust."[72] Commenting on the final, full-colored scene in the Christian graveyard in Jerusalem—a scene that was admired especially by critics who admired the film generally—Mordecai Newman in the *Jewish Frontier* states that the film's last five minutes "comprise as powerful a Holocaust memorial as exists anywhere on earth."[73] Few artifacts of our popular culture have made the journey from Hollywood movie to eternal memorial; fewer still have had so confidently placed upon them such a weight of expectation that they will change the way future generations will conceive of recent history.

For many, finally, the case for *Schindler's List* comes down to the power of the film as a visual statement. Separate from the effect of the film as a whole, the penetrating force of the individual images that Spielberg creates is a source of awe for many reviewers. "With every frame," writes Janet Maslin, "he demonstrates the power of the film maker to distill complex events into fiercely indelible images."[74] The claim that before us is an image that transcends the evanescence of its medium to become indelible is a strong assertion indeed. For

Terrence Rafferty, the force of these visual impressions is such that not only are they indelible but we perceive them as if they are *our own:* these are images that have the "force of intimate experience, the terrible clarity of your own most indelible memories."[75] For Stanley Kauffmann, some of these images, especially ones of children, attain to an iconic status. Like the notorious German army photo of a small Jewish boy, arms upraised, being marched out of the Warsaw Ghetto by soldiers, certain images in *Schindler's List,* like those of the children hiding in the latrines of the Kraków ghetto, are destined to become permanently installed in the "world's memory."[76]

As a visual statement, moreover, *Schindler's List* vindicates the potential of the docudrama, a narrative that presents historical events through their imaginative recreation. The claim for docudramas, beyond their entertainment value, is that they enable us to enter imaginatively into historical events in a way more revealing and intimate than may have been possible at the time they happened. The Holocaust, needless to say, is replete with experiences of horror that no living witnesses survived to describe or that survivors cannot describe. "Throughout the film," for Terrence Rafferty, "Spielberg captures images of experiences that most of us probably thought we would never see presented adequately on the screen."[77] A case in point is the famous shower scene, in which the camera follows a group of naked women being herded into what is ostensibly a gas chamber at Auschwitz-Birkenau; yet, contrary to their worst fears, when the lights go off it is water rather than poison gas that is released from the shower heads. For Rafferty, it is "the most terrifying sequence ever filmed," and he is grateful to this magisterial filmmaker for the visual reevocation that allows him to participate in a memory he could never have had.

A docudrama has to satisfy two standards: historical truthfulness and the ability to do what other media cannot. On the first point, John Gross is persuaded that *Schindler's List* "offers as truthful a picture as we are ever likely to get of regions where no documentary compilation could hope to penetrate."[78] For Robert Galately, a pro-

The Holocaust at the Movies

Oskar Schindler (Liam Neeson) and Nazi SS commandant Amon Geoth (Ralph Fiennes) are presented as opposing studies in good and evil. *Schindler's List*, Universal Pictures

fessor at Western Ontario University, it is not just truthful but approaches being that rare thing: an "adequate" representation in microcosm of the Holocaust as a whole.[79] In the first two isolated shootings in the film, for example, Galately sees a reference to the executions of the mobile killing squads in the East earlier in the war. In the epic struggle between Oskar Schindler and Amon Goeth, he sees dramatized the debate in Nazi policy between *Arbeit*, the exploitation of the Jews through slave labor, and *Vernichtung*, immediate annihilation. It is not just that the movie is inclusive, but in an argument reminiscent of Georg Lukacs's defense of the historical novel, it amounts to a critical representation of historical forces.

Yet it is on the visual and emotive levels that *Schindler's List* declares its qualitative difference from—and superiority to—other form of discursive presentation. "*Schindler's List* is at its best in conveying images and awakening emotions, and in this respect it surpasses straightforward documentaries that give clips of films of the postwar burials in camps like Bergen-Belsen." In a challenge to professional historians, Galately concludes: "In short, the docudrama in the hands of a skilled director is able to evoke dimensions of the Holocaust that could not be communicated through history books, novels, plays, documentary films, or even eyewitness accounts."[80] It is only in Spielberg's hands that the potential of this new art form has so far been realized.

The Critique

The fact that Galately's defense of *Schindler's List* is launched from the pages of an academic journal makes it unusual. Most of the adulatory responses to the movie came in the first wave of reviews with the release of the picture in December 1993, and they appeared in the daily press and in national journals of culture that try to publish their reviews as the films are reaching the public. Negative responses to the film tended to come at a later remove and to appear in academic or intellectual settings. Sometimes there were even "in-house" revisions that signaled a belated depreciation of the film. In the pages of the *New York Times*, Frank Rich dissented from Janet Maslin's delirious review several weeks later.[81] Jason Epstein took issue with John Gross's earlier qualified endorsement of the film in the *New York Review of Books*.[82] The *New Republic*'s literary editor, Leon Wieseltier, used his prerogative to write a column that differed with the positive assessment by the journal's regular film critic, Stanley Kauffmann.[83]

When the negative voices eventually weighed in, the tone was both defensive and aggressive, as if the acclamation for *Schindler's List* had precipitated a general suspension of critical judgment. Michael André Bernstein begins his essay in *The American Scholar* by saying, "There is little pleasure in being troubled by what so many have found deeply moving. For several months now, scarcely a day has gone by without a chorus of impassioned voices, recently augmented by Senator Bill Bradley and California Governor Pete Wilson, publicly testifying to the profound impression Steven Spielberg's film *Schindler's List* made on them personally, while insisting on the movie's educational value for our society as a whole."[84] Added to the chorus is President Clinton, who "implored" the American public to see the movie, according to Philip Gourevitch in *Commentary*. In the encomiums heaped on the film, including its designation as "movie of the year" by *Newsweek* and by film critics' associations in New York and Los Angeles—and one might mention the sweep of the Oscars that took place later that spring—Gourevitch discerns "a kind of cultural grade inflation."[85] What is resented is not so much the weight of all these accolades but the film's success in positioning itself in a category in which any lesser tribute is deemed sacrilege. "[I]t is part of Steven Spielberg's achievement," writes Leon Wieseltier in mock admiration, "to have fulfilled every director's dream, which is to make a film that will bring about a collapse of criticism."[86] It is precisely this exemption from critical evaluation that is rejected by most academic writers and critical intellectuals.[87]

But before hearing the burden of their critique, it is worth reminding ourselves where such views fit into the process of reception, that is, the levels at which a cultural product like a film is disseminated among its consumers. At one level there is the official publicity, which in the case of *Schindler's List* was enormous and included Spielberg's own pronouncements about the film's universal significance, declarations by political leaders, educational screenings, as well as studio handouts and press kits. At another level there are the notices received in the popular press, as described above. At still another level is the experience of ordinary viewers, the tens of millions who went to theaters to see the three-hour-and-five-minute film and then discussed their reactions by word of mouth with friends and in community groups. Finally, there is the rejection of the film by critical intellectuals that will be presently described.

The Holocaust at the Movies

The most elusive of all of these is the response of ordinary viewers. We can read what the studios have passed out and what the critics have written, but when it comes to eavesdropping on the sentiments and perceptions of a mass audience of Americans of all stripes, our usual instruments of measurement are defeated. We are left to rely on what we can deduce from box-office receipts, from the way organs of mass media tend to reflect (as well as create) the will of the people, and finally from the comment that circulates in our own communities. And there are in America many, many communities. It would be enormously enlightening to know how *Schindler's List* was talked about within the hundreds of groups that make up America: among, say, Lutheran church groups in the Midwest, or middle-class African-Americans, or second-generation Korean-Americans.

There is, however, one American group we know something about and whose reactions are especially worthy of attention: Holocaust survivors. From most anecdotal accounts, the reaction of the survivors is echoed in the words of this correspondent, who wrote to *Commentary* magazine to protest Philip Gourevitch's indictment of the film.

> No matter what the critics say, . . . there is only one response, a response usually reserved for another survivor when he concludes giving public testimony. That is appreciatively and warmly to embrace Steven Spielberg in the silent act of bonding.[88]

A similar sentiment is expressed in the name of her mother by film historian Annette Insdorf. Insdorf's mother is a survivor of Bergen-Belsen, Auschwitz, and Plaszow, the last being the camp run by Amon Goeth that is dramatized in the film. Her mother, according to Insdorf, is a sophisticated person, a professor of literature and cinema who is familiar with previous Holocaust films, their imagery and conventions. Yet after seeing *Schindler's List* she was grateful. "She was grateful that the story was told by a popular filmmaker who could get the audience into the theater. She was happy that it was going to be commemorated."[89]

The setting in which Insdorf reports her mother's feeling, the *Village Voice* symposium on the film, is significant. The symposium, whose participants were drawn from film studies and museum work and included the author Art Spiegelman, was held in March 1994, after the initial waves of reviews, Oscar nominations, and stunning public acceptance. The general stance of the symposium's participants toward *Schindler's List* is far from amiable, with Art Spiegelman's acerbic assaults on the film interlacing the critical but more measured observations of the others. It is in the middle of this critique of the film that Insdorf invokes her mother's experience and concludes by saying, "I can't forget her feelings of gratitude at the same time that I allow my critical judgments to enter the picture."[90] This is an important admonition to keep in mind as we examine the intellectuals' case against the movie. There are other, less conspicuous and articulate constituencies whose convictions are just as vehemently held.

It is not what is put in but what is left out of *Schindler's List* that is the point of departure for many critics of the film. *Schindler's List,* they argue, has positioned itself as *the* great cinematic treatment of the Holocaust in our times, and so has it been received by its enormous audience. Yet compared with this presumption, it is contended, Oskar Schindler's story is in fact only a sidelight to the major drama of the Holocaust. Nevertheless, Spielberg brings the story before the public with such mesmerizing and titanic representational force that it subsumes all other narratives and makes the film into the totalizing statement of the Holocaust for most Americans for the foreseeable future. And there is the rub: Spielberg has, in a sense, "won" by powerfully projecting his vision of the Holocaust in the absence of other, more compelling representations.[91]

The indictment of the film begins with the depiction of the Jews. Before the transfer of the surviving Jews to the camp at Plaszow, *Schindler's List* focuses—when it is not preoccupied with Schindler himself—on the behavior of the Jews in the Kraków ghetto. That behavior, argue the critics, consists almost entirely of financial machinations: children swallowing precious stones, nervy young black marketeers making deals, stolid elders of the Jewish council producing stacks of bank notes to back Schindler's factory. While these stratagems for economic survival certainly took place and deserve no censure, they have been exclusively selected over other behaviors to represent Jewish life in the ghetto. Jews engaged in a wide variety of cultural expressions, as described in the previous chapter, including writing poetry, producing plays and cabarets, putting out newspapers, and teaching religious texts. Many of these activities were continuations, fragmentary under the circumstances, of the rich, centuries-long cultural life of East European Jewry. Rather than each family's being caught up in hiding its wealth, there was an extensive network of private and communal welfare and mutual aid institutions and organizations. Far from smuggling being the only form of resistance, moreover, there was intense political organizing taking place in the ghetto with contacts made with resistance groups in the countryside.

The exclusion of these forms of Jewish collective self-expression must be laid, it is argued, squarely at Spielberg's door. The Keneally book upon which the film is based is aware of these activities; Spielberg, and his screenwriter, Steven Zaillian, chose otherwise. When the Jews are not busy hiding money or making deals, they blur into an anonymous mass of victims. Aside from Stern, there are no Jewish characters in the film who either take any action or are distinguished in their individuality. And Stern himself, who is credited in Keneally's volume with an active role in saving the *Schindlerjuden,* is reduced in the film to the role of an admiring sidekick. All individuality and personality are sucked up by Schindler, in whose imperial presence the Jews are mostly small, nameless automatons. For a film that was supposed to signal Spielberg's return to his Jewish identity, observes Gourevitch, "*Schindler's List* depicts the Nazi slaughter of Polish Jewry almost entirely through German eyes."[92] It thus reinforces a conception of the Holocaust as the narrative of the perpetrators rather than that of the victims.[93]

Particular offense is given by a scene that does not even appear in the book: a gathering of Jewish men in the Kraków cathedral to conduct black-market transactions. The men dip their fingers into holy water upon entering, and while making believe they are participating in the Latin mass, they trade in silk shirts, chocolates, and hosiery. In this and other instances, writes Sara Horowitz, "the film reproduces the anti-Semitic stereotype of the crafty, canny, well-connected Jews, as promulgated in the *Protocols of the Elders of Zion*."[94] This church scene—there is a later one in which Schindler renews his vows to his wife—is heightened by mythic religious overtones, argues Horowitz. The scene "resonates with the New Testament's multiple descriptions of Jews defiling the Temple and Jesus's consequent need to purify the holy space by throwing out the Jewish money changers (Matt. 21:12–13, Mark 11:15–17, Luke 19:45–46)."[95] The profanation of sacred space confirms the image of the Jews as materialistic and avaricious, and it is only a Christian who can recall them to their spirituality. In another scene, which takes place later in the film after his conversion, Schindler reminds a rabbi among his workers that it is the Jewish Sabbath and that he should attend to its observance.

The second major criticism of *Schindler's List* is both the most predictable and most damning: the movie never escapes the conventions of the Hollywood feature film. The plot is melodramatic. The movie relies on sentiment and manipulates its viewers, and it is centered on a heroic individual who saves the day and delivers the necessary happy ending. Now, the murder of European Jewry is a world-shattering event and the greatest eruption of evil in our time. Yet rather than exploding the received genres of popular entertainment—or at least testing their limits—*Schindler's List* keeps within the bounds of its Hollywood origins. This artistic timidity in the eyes of the critics becomes more than a simple failure of nerve when the subject is the Holocaust. It amounts to a vulgarization of something profoundly tragic and to a betrayal of the millions of victims who were not saved.

The Holocaust at the Movies

Schindler saves many of the children of his factory workers by convincing an SS guard that their small hands are needed to polish the insides of artillery casings. *Schindler's List*

This last point should be made first. Of the very many stories, both collective and individual, that Spielberg could have chosen to make his definitive statement about the Holocaust, he chose the most marginal and exotic: a Nazi/Christian rescuer. In taking issue with an earlier, favorable review of the film by John Gross in the *New York Review of Books*, Jason Epstein writes in the same journal that, while good deeds in evil times should certainly be celebrated, Spielberg has done something on a very different scale of misrepresentation.

He has placed the oddity Schindler in the foreground of his tale and let him determine the triumphant outcome. But Schindler's good deed was marginal and its motive obscure, so different from the behavior of countless others at the time as to suggest that he might have come from a different planet, like another famous Spielberg character.[96]

What Schindler did affected no one except for his workers and made no difference to the outcome of the Holocaust. The real problem, Epstein argues, is not Schindler's oddity but the implication that "remarkable individuals can outsmart evil."

> What then of the others? Did they die by the millions simply because they weren't clever enough themselves or lucky enough to find a Schindler of their own? Does the film mean to suggest that if only there had been enough Schindlers, the problem of evil which the Holocaust raises would have been solved, that it was merely for lack of cleverness or luck on the part of the victims that they died?[97]

Together with numbers of other critics of the film, Epstein sees in Spielberg's fundamental choice of material an intuitive resistance to the dark core of the Holocaust.[98] It is not that Spielberg's intentions are necessarily commercial or exploitative. Rather, despite his being a superior film technician—or perhaps because of it—he remains, in Geoffrey Hartman's phrase, a "cinema animal," a creature of the Hollywood world he has helped to make and whose limitations he has no desire to challenge. He is provoked by the tremendum of the Holocaust to do the same thing that has always been done, even if he does it better than others and with more gravity. The Hollywood imperative remains untouched: move viewers through cycles of dread and relief, give them a larger-than-life adventure to identify with, and in the end, of course, leave them with a sense of uplift.

The movie-ness of *Schindler's List* cuts in two directions. On the one hand, its debt to previous popular movies is evident throughout. For example, in the scene in which Schindler, Christlike, delivers a sermon to the awestruck Jews looking up at him from the floor of the Brinnlitz factory, Michael Andre Bernstein sees "a direct crib from every sand-and-sandals epic from *The Ten Commandments* and

The Holocaust at the Movies

Ben Hur to *Jesus Christ Superstar.*"[99] On the other hand, *Schindler's List* seeks to evade its status as a Hollywood drama by presenting itself as an authentic, even vintage documentary. Shooting on black-and-white stock, filming with handheld cameras, and staging the action on location in Poland or on sets that are reconstructed with painstaking accuracy—all these are effects that are designed, in Leon Wieseltier's words, to make the film "look like a restored print of itself" rather than a recent release from Amblin Entertainment, Spielberg's production company.[100] To reinforce the documentary effect, moreover, *Schindler's List* contains filmic quotations from and allusions to true documentaries such as Claude Lanzmann's *Shoah* and Alain Resnais's *Night and Fog*.[101] These efforts to create verisimilitude, in the eyes of the film's critics, are not signs merely of industrious filmmaking and a responsibility to historical detail. It is taken rather as a kind of dissimulation whereby the viewer is invited "to imagine that one is looking at the Holocaust itself, or at a film taken at the time."[102] Now, while this may be a tribute to the powers of Spielberg's visual imagination, it is a dangerous illusion because of the exceedingly biased way in which this historical simulacrum is constituted and because of grimmer and more disturbing realities that are left out.

The greatest point of contention is the figure of Schindler himself. There is a principled resentment, as we have already seen, of the very weight Schindler displaces within the economy of the film. This tall matinee idol towers over the Jews and dominates the action. His appetites energize the narrative. The lives and the deaths of the Jewish victims are refracted through his point of view. In short, he sucks up representation. Separate from the question of dominance, however, is the question of motive. Spielberg's refusal to explore the reasons for Schindler's conversion, which is taken as a supreme act of modesty and restraint by the film's advocates, is taken by its critics as a supreme act of evasion. As an alternative to Spielberg's silence, Philip Gourevitch points to the portrayal of Schindler in Keneally's book, which is presumably closer to the historical record. Keneally's

The Holocaust at the Movies

Schindler reacts to seeing the liquidation of the Kraków ghetto by inwardly renouncing Nazism and resolving to do everything in his power to defeat the system. He is motivated by "disgust, which is to say a sense of common humanity."[103] The commonness of Schindler's humanity, moreover, is brought out in the alcoholism, bankruptcy, and unhappy profligacy that marked his life after the war, a period covered in the book but not the film. Spielberg's revision of Keneally's Schindler strips him of his "human complexity and replaces it with—nothing." "By robbing us of Schindler's renunciation of Nazism," Gourevitch concludes, "Spielberg gives us a simply enigmatic creation, the good Nazi."[104]

Among the Hollywood conventions that Spielberg is least willing to part with, according to his detractors, is the intimate connection between violence and sexuality. Despite the high calling and supreme sensitivity supposedly embodied in the making of the film, *Schindler's List* carries over the same eroticization of female victimhood found in many lesser, exploitative films on the Holocaust and in the general run of Hollywood entertainments. For some viewers, like Molly Magid Hoagland in the pages of the Jewish journal *Midstream*, Spielberg's is a sad moral failure. "We are justified in demanding the highest possible standards of respect and good taste in the depiction of our family tragedy."[105] The bared breasts of Schindler's and Goeth's mistresses are unnecessary to establish the powerfulness of their Aryan lovers. When it comes to the Jewish victims, Sara Horowitz sees this same "appeal to the audience's voyeurism" repeated in the shower scene at Auschwitz, which she terms "pornographic both for its depiction of terrified, naked Jewish women and for its use of the gas chamber to provoke the viewer's sense of suspense."[106] The relations between the Germans and their female Jewish victims are more complex because of the status of Jews as nonpersons and the prohibition of sexual contact between the two. Amon Goeth desires Helen Hirsch, the beautiful Jewish inmate he takes as a servant, and although he might shoot her, he will not sleep with her. His desire is enacted, according to

Horowitz, through the rifle he keeps at his side, which he uses to shoot Jews randomly from the balcony of his villa overlooking the Plaszow camp. Now, wanton sexuality was indeed part of Nazi domination, as was the ideologically charged stereotyping of women, both Jewish and Aryan; and *Schindler's List* provided Spielberg with an opportunity to critically expose this historically embedded complex of attitudes. "But Spielberg's film does not advance such a critique," argues Horowitz; "rather, it simply absorbs and reproduces these images of women and violence, without knowingly interrupting or interrogating their production."[107]

The final plank in the critique of *Schindler's List* concerns what philosophers and critics call the crisis of representation. Given the unprecedented transcendent horror of the Holocaust, can it or should it be represented in language and art? The distinction between "can" and "should" takes the question in two directions. The first addresses the adequacy of language and art to communicate the enormity of the evil without simply containing it in preexisting categories; it further questions the very efficacy of direct depictions of atrocity. The second direction raises moral issues. Representations of Holocaust violence inevitably privilege the perpetrators rather than the victims and abet a voyeuristic fascination with evil that often bears an erotic-pornographic charge. When it comes to depicting the ultimate dehumanization of the victims in the killing machinery in a mode that is not strictly documentary—fiction or drama, for example—this is simply a place conscience tells us we have no right to go.[108]

It is just this kind of violation that Spielberg's detractors charge him with. He confidently takes his cameras into the horror of horrors without the slightest awareness of the problems of what he is doing. Yet for Spielberg there are no "traces of difficulty," remarks Leon Wieseltier. "Very robustly Spielberg just barrels through," bringing his camera through the door of the showers/gas chamber at Auschwitz. There are limits to what can be depicted, and for Wieseltier, that "point is the door." One of the ghastliest sights touched on in *Schindler's List* is the outdoor pits in which thousands of bodies were burned.

> Anybody who has seen photographs of films of these fiery, open-air charnels knows that the camera has probably never recorded a sight more obscene. But here was a director, and wardrobe and makeup, poring over the tone of charred flesh, the hollowing of rotted skulls, the disposition of mangled bones, to get it right. What on earth did they think they were doing? Do they really think that they got it right?[109]

Ever since the Holocaust intellectuals have famously debated whether there can be art in the aftermath of the catastrophe. "What Spielberg has shown the world," remarks film professor Gertrud Koch sardonically in the *Village Voice* symposium, "is there is nothing that can't be narrated."[110]

Yet paralyzed silence is not the only alternative to Spielberg's robust and mindless barreling through. Commentators point to Claude Lanzmann's documentary film *Shoah* as an example of a viable other path. Lanzmann's film, which was released in 1985, is well known for its rigorous exclusions. Lanzmann declines to use either documentary footage from the war years or dramatic recreations of the events of the Holocaust. He relies instead on lengthy, probing interviews with survivors and non-Jewish bystanders, with the addition of footage shot in contemporary Eastern Europe of rail lines and the ruins of concentration camps. With its "talking heads" and its nine-hour-and-twenty-three-minute length, *Shoah* is not a film intended for a mass audience, and indeed, even though it is widely known among serious viewers, the disproportion between the number of people who have see *Shoah* and *Schindler's List* is astronomical. Lanzmann's own reactions to Spielberg's movie have been widely reported. Although he professes great respect for Spielberg's earlier work, he takes issue with Spielberg's decision to focus almost all the action through Schindler's eyes. But even if Spielberg had

devised a more successful strategy, Lanzmann would not in principle entertain the very conception of the enterprise.

> The Holocaust is above all unique in that it erects a ring of fire around
> itself, a borderline that cannot be crossed because there is a certain
> ultimate degree of horror that cannot be transmitted. To claim it is
> possible to do so is to be guilty of the most serious transgression.
> Fiction is a transgression. I deeply believe there are some things that
> cannot and should not be represented.[111]

If not all critics have been drawn to the profoundly moralistic tone
of Lanzmann's declaration, many have championed his practice in
his documentary work. Lanzmann's principled restraints have
avoided, they claim, the dangers of kitsch and trivialization inescapable in the enterprise of restaging the real-life events of the
Holocaust. Lanzmann is thus saved from falling into the trap
described by Art Spiegelman in a phrase whose pithiness has given
it great currency: "the problem of re-creation for the sake of the
audience's recreation."[112]

Now, to say that *Shoah* escapes the conventions of Hollywood
moviemaking is not to say that it is a film innocent of artifice. Omer
Bartov reminds us of Lanzmann's cagey astuteness in choosing the
kind of interviewees who would either unwittingly incriminate
themselves (if they were bystanders) or arrive at an unanticipated
emotional catharsis (if they were survivors). Lanzmann's dramatiza-
tion of himself as an omnipresent figure in his own film calls attention to the tactical manipulation of each of his subjects. Finally, there
is the presumption on Lanzmann's part—which is parallel to
Spielberg's own—that his film represents a kind of ultimate reck-
oning with the Holocaust.[113] Taken together, these aspects of the
film are not "problems" that vitiate Lanzmann's achievement, but
they do indicate that *Shoah*, like all strong works of art, is, in its own
way, deeply troped and worthy of critical investigation. Yet the debate
over *Schindler's List* has led to what Miriam Bratu Hansen calls a

The Holocaust at the Movies

"binary opposition of *Schindler's List* and *Shoah*" in which the apotheosis of the latter has prevented attention to the "material and textual specificity" of the former.[114]

In the end, the issue of the representability of the Holocaust can be tested only by artists who fashion representations that are persuasive enough to beg the question. The vehemence of the opposition to *Schindler's List* can be explained only by the film's power. Where, in the end, does this power reside? For critical viewers who can factor out the Hollywood elements of suspense, sex, and heroic action (although these are admittedly not small exclusions), the film's power—and thus its threat—lies in the artistry of Spielberg's visual imagination. What Spielberg does with the fifteen-minute sequence of the liquidation of the Kraków ghetto is begrudgingly conceded even by harsh critics as visually brilliant. The camera seems to be everywhere: in the midst of the chaos in the ghetto, high on the bluffs taking the action in whole from Schindler's perspective, in the frenzied throngs, as well as in discrete apartments and courtyards registering arresting individual moments. The sequence is shocking in its sense of reality, and it would take a full-scale analysis of the film techniques deployed to account for Spielberg's success in achieving this reality effect. The success is stunning, and that's the rub for the critics: it is too real.

We have an urgent need to imagine the Holocaust, while at the same time we have a poverty of images. We, the belated bystanders, were not there, and no matter how familiar we are with the facts and the lore of the Holocaust, we have only some grainy footage shot by the Nazis with which to feed our visual memories. This is true in a sense for survivors themselves, even for survivors of the Kraków ghetto, for no individual victim could possess the omniscient and protean knowledge available to Spielberg's camera as it takes in both the collective trauma and the many parallel lives of the victims. In the absence of a visual record, then, writes Elazar Barkan, the most affecting and effective scenes in *Schindler's List* "become our new memories" and "will now serve as historical

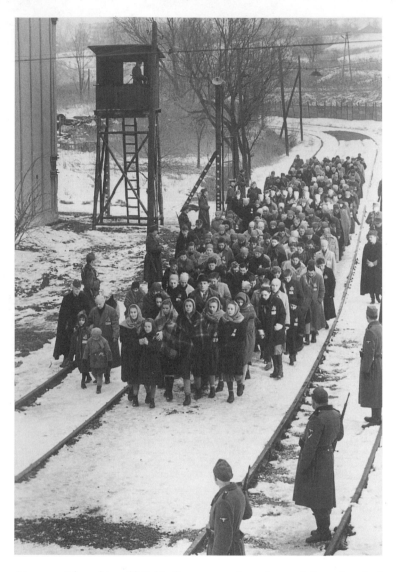

At great risk to himself, Schindler secures the release of three hundred of his factory women and children, who had been accidentally sent to Auschwitz-Birkenau. *Schindler's List*

knowledge."[115] Spielberg has given our knowledge visual concreteness, and he has done it so effectively that his staging of historical events has installed itself in our minds as the way things happened. We will remember them in Spielberg's version if only to deviate from it. For Spielberg's admirers, this is evidence of his magisterial achievement; for his detractors it is evidence of a colossal and subversive arrogation of power.

An American Debate

Having reviewed the arguments for and against *Schindler's List*, I look back and become aware that my account is not, despite my best efforts, entirely evenhanded. I have given more space to the critics rather than the advocates and have allowed their views to be articulated with more rhetorical intensity. I belong, in the end, to the cadres of "critical intellectuals," and my own biases cannot, it would seem, be wholly suppressed. Yet what most interests me—and what constitutes the larger aim of this inquiry in its whole and in its parts— is not arriving at a judgment or fashioning a critical position concerning this film or other films or any response to the Holocaust. It is rather the project of understanding how these cultural products reflect and provoke American thinking and American attitudes. *Schindler's List*, whether one likes the film or not, is a strong work of popular culture that has elicited a widespread engagement with the Holocaust, or at least certain aspects of it, in the public cultural discourse of America. Whether the impact of the film brought new attitudes into play or catalyzed a reconfiguration of existing ones may be impossible to determine. What can be said for certain is that the reception of Spielberg's film tells us a great deal about the terms on which a mass American audience was willing to admit the Holocaust into the "mainstream" of its consciousness fifty years after the tragedy and at lesser removes from earlier depictions of the event in film and television.

At the core of the debate, to begin with, is the individualism of the Schindler figure. Schindler—and his doppelganger, Amon Goeth—absorb the Jews and the Germans around them into their towering, charismatic, and individual presences. There is, to be sure, a long tradition in American cinema of strong leading men, either romantic or demonic, and Schindler's matinee-idol quality helps him to fit comfortably into the practices and expectations of Americans at the movies. And it is easy to see Oskar Schindler taking his place in the line of Indiana Jones and other resourceful and intrepid heroes in Spielberg's earlier films. Yet on a separate moral and political level, this individual formation speaks to a deeper set of American attitudes, not just about the Holocaust but about the place of the individual in America.

Nazism may have been an eruption of radical evil, but it was also uncontestably a set of social and political processes that overtook a whole society, and the murder of European Jewry was, similarly, an enterprise that was accomplished in stages and through multiple procedures. It is not that *Schindler's List* oversimplifies the historical record, which is an unavoidable consequence of making history into a screenplay, but that Spielberg chooses to collapse collective behavior into individual action. The myriad of ways in which the Jews came upon their fate and responded to it—the whole range from resistance and concealment to mutual aid and collaboration—finds almost no place in the film. The Jews are a mass, a bloc, but not a collective, a people. As for the Germans, we see nothing of the "ordinary" Germans (or Poles or Ukrainians or Romanians) who formed the police battalions in the East or who administered Nazi justice in the courts (as in *Judgment at Nuremberg*) or who happily moved into expropriated Jewish property and businesses. The whole German reality during the war is devolved into Schindler's (unexplained) goodness and Goeth's (unexplained) evil.

This arrangement has the indisputable advantage of relieving American viewers of the need to take responsibility for the Holocaust as a German issue. A comparison with *Judgment at Nuremberg* is telling. Unlike *Schindler's List,* Stanley Kramer's 1961 movie reopened the question of German collective responsibility for the concentration camps and focused on the corruption of justice at the middle rather than at the highest levels of the Nazi regime. Yet in a way that is analogous to Spielberg's film, *Judgment at Nuremberg* ends by abstracting and generalizing the question of justice such that it reverberates from Germany back to America. The ideal of justice in America, though ultimately defensible, remains continually vulnerable to political expediency and to the self-serving fading of historical memory.

There is an enormous consolation in the dual conviction that individuals move history and that the goodness or evil incarnated within them is beyond our comprehension. Americans have long nurtured the notion that individuals can make their own fate and defeat the limitations placed upon them by membership in a collective, be it a class, a religion, or a racial or ethnic group. Schindler is a savior and Goeth a monster in Spielberg's film, yet they share the way in which their exceptionality pushes everything else and everyone else to the margins of representation. We may identify sympathetically with Schindler's goodness, as we may be fascinated by Goeth's monstrosity; yet few of us would see ourselves as world-historical individuals invested with extreme moral essences. This is our consolation. Like the Jews and the Germans depicted in the film, we live in a world riven by seemingly intractable forces of good and evil, and like them, our power to influence those forces is feeble. Yet there exist historical actors, be their motives obscure, who do battle over us or for us, and although evil almost always has the upper hand, there are moments when we are rescued.

Rescue is a second theme that underlies the reception of *Schindler's List* at many levels. The film's "happy ending" was an easy target for the film's critics to ridicule as a Hollywood staple. Yet the issue is more profound than the use of a conventional plot device. The American audience will not accept—and certainly not accept with accolades—the story about the true fate of the overwhelming majority of European Jews. No more now than during the celebration of the victory over Nazism immediately after the war is the generality of Americans willing to sustain an unmitigated and unrelieved vision of suffering and atrocity. This is true not only for the Jews but for such other "absolute" victims as the Cambodians and the Rwandans. What has changed for many Americans—and here too through the dissemination of other works of popular culture—is an increased level of general awareness of the brute facts of the Holocaust. Spielberg does not have to educate and inform his audience about the implementation of the Final Solution the way the 1978 television miniseries had to. For at least part of his audience, Spielberg can assume this knowledge to be part of their "competence" as viewers and therefore give himself leave to embed within the master narrative of the Holocaust the "peripheral" story of Schindler and the Jews he saved. That the story of this tiny and atypical pocket of deliverance is located within the overwhelmingly tragic frame that contains it goes without saying. But in the American context it can, perhaps, be no other way.

The foregrounding of rescue also reflects a deep shift in American attitudes concerning the Jewish victims of the Holocaust. In the decades after the war, as Alvin Rosenfeld has pointed out, it was the Jews who were killed and the Nazis who killed them—and the bystanders to these crimes, as well—who were understood to have played the central roles in the historical drama of the Holocaust, to the degree that these matters were openly discussed at all.[116] During the past twenty years or so, the dyad of victim–perpetrator has been moved to the sidelines by the emergence of another pairing: survivor-rescuer. The change is a profound one, and as was suggested in chapter 1, its determinants are manifold. The self-assertion of the survivors, the advocacy of their children (the "Second Generation"), Elie Wiesel's leadership as a public figure—these were among the factors in the extraordinary rehabilitation of the survivor in the American mind. The newly elevated status of the survivors led to a new interest in and an eventual ennoblement of those gentiles who helped to make survival possible: the Catholic Poles who hid individual families, the French villages that abetted escape, the American GIs who liberated the camps, and heroic individuals such as Raoul Wallenberg, Shugihara, and Schindler himself. The elevation of the survivor-rescuer paradigm reached its apotheosis at the Academy Awards ceremony in 1994 in which Steven Spielberg, with coproducer and survivor Branko Lustig by his side, held his Oscar aloft and accepted his award on behalf of all the survivors of the Holocaust.

This shift of emphasis, so powerfully projected by *Schindler's List,* is the result not just of the survivors' activism; it also reflects a deep receptivity on the part of the American audience to the idea and message of rescue. As Lawrence Langer has never ceased pointing out, it is the nature of the American mind, and perhaps human nature in general, to avoid abiding the unremittingly tragic.[117] To focus attention on the six million Jewish victims who were killed rather than on the small number of victims who survived, to contemplate the mechanism of annihilation and the suffering it induced, to behold the ultimate degradation of men and women and the idea of humanity, and to stay with this knowledge, refusing to be diverted by redemptive consolations that come in many forms—this is an enormous challenge that few can meet with any constancy. Tales of survival and rescue, while stirring and significant in themselves, Langer argues, have the potential to afford our minds refuge from the difficulty of abiding the fate of the six million. In a lush and elaborate way, *Schindler's List* provides just such an opportunity. It is not cynical to observe that a movie focusing on the mass murder of European Jewry, even if it were made by a director of Spielberg's talents, would not secure a large following. The vast success of *Schindler's List* signifies and confirms a kind of compact between Spielberg and his audience that makes a statement to this effect: The Holocaust as a subject may move to the center of public awareness on the condition that it has a message of affirmation to offer us.

The good news embodied in the idea of rescue also has an unmistakable theological dimension. Rescue means redemption and redemption means hope, and this is a notion that is congenial to more than one religious group in America. Of all the stories of the Holocaust through which to make his major statement, Spielberg chose a story about a rescuer, and of all the stories about rescuers he chose one about a fallen Christian who returns to his faith and saves himself by saving Jews. It is worth recalling that there are two church scenes in *Schindler's List*. In the first, Jewish black marketeers pretend to say mass as they transact business; in the second, Schindler seeks forgiveness from his wife for his womanizing and rededicates himself to their marriage. The absence of an explanation for Schindler's moral regeneration opens the door to a theological construction; it is neither striving nor a tortured conscience but the operation of grace that has turned about the course of his life. The prevalence of water that brings deliverance (the hosing down of the suffocating cattle car and the shower scene) provides the narrative with an identifiable mythic Christian motif for those who want to see it.[118] Not only does Schindler save Jews but he encourages them to be better Jews. In his Sermon on the Mount in Brinnlitz he teaches a doctrine of forgiveness and the renunciation of violence.

It has not gone unnoticed, as we have seen, that for all that has been said about Spielberg's return to his Jewishness through the making of this film, the film itself puts the Jews in the background and places a Christian hero and his act of salvation at the center.[119] *Schindler's List* thus gives American Christian viewers a way they can feel comfortable with approaching a subject that in the past has been fraught with blame. Instead of Christianity's being charged with evasion of responsibility during the war or even being held accountable for laying the doctrinal groundwork for the murderous rage against the Jews, Christian faith is depicted in the film as a force that makes for deliverance. Being identified with a process of redemption in the context of the Holocaust is the way Christians, I take leave to imagine, would most like to see themselves; and Spielberg's film allows them to do that. With that capacity in hand, *Schindler's List* creates an ecumenical cultural space in which Jews and Christians can come together around one of the most traumatic events of modern history. The Jewish community, a small American minority, is deeply gratified and confirmed by a great motion picture being made about a catastrophe that it regards its own[120]; the Christian community, the great majority in an America that is only partly secular, is pleased to be given the chance to have its teachings portrayed favorably rather than being tinged with culpability. The occasions in America for moral consensus across ethnic and religious lines are few. The enormous success of *Schindler's List* is evidence of the enormity of that aspiration.

What is redeemed in the end through the agency of this movie—and this is the third and final American theme—is nothing less than the medium of the moving image itself. Movies are the offspring of the marriage between technology and entertainment, and there has been no more successful fruit of that union than Steven Spielberg's work. Through films like *Jaws, E. T., Close Encounters of the Third Kind,* and the Indiana Jones trilogy, Spielberg deployed the increasingly sophisticated techniques available to filmmakers to engender effects of fear, suspense, and fantasy and thus produce superior entertainments. Yet despite their virtuosity, these films never succeeded in becoming more than superior entertainments for the reason that their moral vision was arrested in an adolescent moment of adventure and escape. *Schindler's List* is Spielberg's breakthrough film because through it he transcends the boy's fascination with his toys and his need to please and mobilizes his talents on behalf of a theme of high seriousness. Because Spielberg is one of the most powerful and closely observed figures in Hollywood, the biographical significance of his Holocaust film was quickly noted and widely celebrated. *Schindler's List,* wrote Stephen Schiff in a *New Yorker* profile, "has had the effect of a giant bar mitzvah, a rite of passage. Prince Hal has become Henry V; the dauphin has emerged a king."[121]

The Holocaust at the Movies

Spielberg's Holocaust film also signaled his affirmation of Judaism, fatherhood, and family life. The rediscovery of his Jewishness was triggered, according to his own testimony in numerous interviews, by his exposure to the Holocaust. In the aftermath of the film, this rekindled interest was institutionalized in the work of two foundations he established. One gives out grants to promote Jewish identity and advance the ideal of tolerance that Spielberg sees as the essential teaching of the Holocaust; the other is a vast project aimed at collecting video testimony from Holocaust survivors and preserving it in a digitized archive for the use of future generations. In his personal life, Spielberg publicly rejected the glitzy high life of Hollywood movie barons and committed himself to a strong and stable family life and to participation in raising his children.

Was it the Holocaust that accomplished all this? In the absence of more probing and critical biographical and autobiographical reflection, it is difficult to know whether it was the making of the film that led to the realignment of his life or whether it was the other way around. But when it comes to the autobiographical myth attached to *Schindler's List* and amplified in the media, it is the Holocaust that is pointed to as the evident catalyst for change. Spielberg had come of age as an artist, as a Jew, and as a husband/father, and his "return" and his "reform" were credited to his engagement with the destruction of European Jewry.

The possibility for elevation extends beyond Spielberg's life to his métier as a film director and beyond that to the vocation of the moving image itself. Within the film industry, the triumph of *Schindler's List*—as measured by the sweep of the Academy Awards but not by that measure alone—was taken not just as a marker of Spielberg's coming of age but as a sign of the vindication of the redemptive potential of American popular film as a whole. Here was a movie—not an art film but a Hollywood movie—that transcends the imparting of good feelings and good values, the upper limits of aspiration hitherto ascribed to the products of the industry. In the words of Jeffrey Katzenberg, who at the time ran the

The Holocaust at the Movies

Walt Disney film studios, "I think *Schindler's List* will wind up being so much more important than a movie. It will affect how people on this planet think and act. At a moment in time, it is going to remind us about the dark side, and do it in a way in which, whenever that little green monster is lurking somewhere, this movie is going to press it down again. I don't want to burden the movie too much, but I think it will bring peace on earth, good will to men. Enough of the right people will see it that it will actually set the course of world affairs."[122] Even after these words are adjusted for the inflation endemic to the industry, they break new ground as to the moral horizons that can be claimed or even thought about on behalf of the movies.

And not just the movies but the very notion of visuality in the American mode. In this view, the apotheosis of *Schindler's List* has definitively settled the artistic agon between the anti-iconography of Claude Lanzmann with its interdictions on direct representation and the American preference for dramatic recreations of historical events. Spielberg's successful deployment of the techniques of visualization on behalf of events that had been thought to be unrepresentable means that there is nowhere the moving image cannot go without the fear of moral betrayal.

From the myth of Spielberg's career there emerges, then, a new and major role for the Holocaust to play in American culture: the Holocaust as an agent of moral seriousness that changes people's lives for the better and confers on the American popular mind the possibility of escape from vulgarity. This amelioration is not for Jews alone. For Jews it may indeed take the form of a deeper attachment to Jewish values and Jewish identity; for non-Jews and for Americans in general it may take the form of a deeper tolerance for cultural, religious, and ethnic differences, and it may also simply recall us to our best selves by reminding us of what is of ultimate importance and what is not.

The fact that America derives this significant moral benefit from the Holocaust does not mean that it proposes to give nothing back in return. As the generation of the survivors passes away and the possibility of authentic witness dims, it is precisely the American genius for visual representation that is looked to, if not for salvation, then at least for a reprieve from the drift of forgetfulness. Whether the American way with the moving image, as docudrama or video archive, will be able to repay this debt of gratitude in the future remains an open question.

4

The Future of Memorialization

Are Americans preoccupied with the Holocaust? Are they overly preoccupied with the Holocaust? These are difficult questions to answer, although I shall try to do so shortly. Yet let us grant for the moment that the Holocaust is indeed much on the minds of Americans, at least in comparison to its marginality several decades ago. If that is the case, then what will happen when the Holocaust loses its centrality in our public discourse? If the examples discussed in this volume have had anything to teach, it is a lesson about how the remembrance of the Holocaust in America is wrapped around a changing mix of ulterior motives. The mix is destined to shift, although no one can foresee precisely in what ways, and the Holocaust will surely be enlisted for different ends and most probably lose some of its heat as a topic in American culture. The pace at which museums and memorials are being erected will moderate, and the flood of memoirs will slow to a trickle as the survivors pass away.

On that day it will behoove us to be ready with an answer to the question of what we—to the degree that it is in our power to determine—want the remembrance of the Holocaust to be. James Young has wisely noted the difference between collective memory, an organic process through which a community's relationship to its past is developed, and memorialization, a purposeful process in which

The Future of Memorialization

a community endeavors to determine its relationship to the past.[1] The interplay between these two complex processes is itself complex and will form the subject of later exploration. It is enough for now to use these two terms in a very simple sense to characterize the present moment in the following way. In the last two decades of the twentieth century, the instances of Holocaust remembrance—documents, photographs, memoirs, memorials, museums, films, movies—have been so numerous and so intense and so chaotically all-encompassing as to leave little room for the intentionality and self-awareness of memorialization. But as this intensity wanes, as it is likely to do, a space will be opened up for thoughtful reflection on how we—the "we" being the diverse and plural communities of America—wish to construct the future of Holocaust memory on these shores.

I use the notion of constructing memory deliberately to mark a shift in my argument from the descriptive to the prescriptive. When in chapter 2 I compared the constructivist and exceptionalist positions in the study of Holocaust representation, my purpose was to clarify the difference between two major explanatory models; and if I favored the former over the latter, it was for the contructivist model's greater power to discriminate among the varieties of responses to the Holocaust. In this concluding set of reflections, I put aside the constructivist position as an analytic tool for understanding records of Holocaust culture and take it up instead as a guide to thinking about the future—as a policy-planning tool, as it were—and to considering the question of how we want to remember the Holocaust. I shall first examine the issues in the debate concerning the excessive preoccupation with the Holocaust in American Jewish life and the necessarily mixed nature of the motivations involved. The second subject is the dynamics of memorialization and the process whereby different communities shape different relationships to Holocaust memory. The resources for the construction of this memory, especially the problematic use of videotaped survivor testimony, will form the matter of the conclusion.

The Future of Memorialization

ARE AMERICAN JEWS PREOCCUPIED
WITH THE HOLOCAUST?

The gathering prominence of the Holocaust in American life has been matched by a gathering critique of that prominence. I refer not to Holocaust denial, a serious phenomenon whose proportions are hard to measure; that is part of another discussion. I refer instead to views articulated within the American Jewish community that argue that the preeminence of the Holocaust has been achieved at the expense of support for issues more vital to the future of Judaism and the Jewish people. It is "within the family" of the Jewish community that critical reservations about Holocaust-centeredness have been most freely expressed. Such reservations, or even resistance, may abound in general, non-Jewish circles in American culture; yet the powerful moral prestige of the Holocaust, I suspect, often prevents these thoughts from being aired. But because most American Jews view the Holocaust as a concern that ultimately belongs to them, they are more ready to engage in debate, even though the constraints deriving from the solemnity of the subject are hardly put aside. We will take up the critique as it comes from different quarters of the community.

To begin with, focusing on destruction is not what Jewish life is about, according to the synagogue movements in American life, and this can be said with variations concerning the branches of Reform, Conservative, and Orthodox Judaism altogether. Judaism is, in the main, a religion at whose core lies observing the commandments, studying the Torah, keeping the Sabbath, hallowing the rites of passage in the life cycle, public worship, and contributing to the upbuilding of the Land of Israel. There is without doubt a religious imperative to mourn the destruction of Jerusalem and later catastrophes and never to forget the evil deeds of Amalek in their contemporaneous manifestations throughout the ages. Yet the sway of the tragic strain within Judaism is limited; it is integrated into fixed points in the daily liturgy and the yearly rhythm of the sacred cal-

The Future of Memorialization

endar. Even if it is acknowledged that the Holocaust stands apart and warrants its own ritual occasions, those observances should stand as a supplement to, rather than a substitution for, the positive content of Jewish religious life.

The foundational events of Judaism remain the Exodus from Egypt and the Revelation of the Torah at Sinai—however differently they are interpreted by different outlooks. As an instance of negative transcendence, the destruction of European Jewry is certainly a terrible mystery, but it does not warrant the status of an event upon which an equivalent structure of meaning can be erected. By presenting itself as a religion of suffering and martyrdom, moreover, Judaism thus presents itself to Christianity and the world in a way that is not true to itself.

Second, transmitting the heritage of Judaism to the next generation of Jews is the mission of Jewish education, and that mission has never been more severely tested than in the last decades of the twentieth century. The secular American culture that surrounds young people and dominates their lives—consumerism, entertainment, sports, professional achievement, personal gratification—makes it very difficult to find an opening through which the teachings of Judaism and the history of the Jewish people can be meaningfully introduced. Yet there is an antidote, for it is only the most hardened teenager who remains unaffected by being shown films about the Holocaust or even by being taken to visit the extermination sites in Europe. Because these scenes of pathos and atrocity often have the power to trigger a strong visceral reaction, exposure to the Holocaust is prone to being mobilized as the last functioning weapon in the arsenal of Jewish education. The use of the Holocaust in this way thus represents not so much the success of Jewish historical memory as the failure to convey the real contents of Jewish literacy.

Third, from secularist-culturalist Jews, for whom the Yiddish language embodies the great civilization of Eastern Europe, the preoccupation with the Holocaust receives a distinctly mixed welcome. At the very least, the murder of the Jews of Eastern Europe creates an awareness of the fact that there were vast numbers of Jews who lived in Eastern Europe *before* they were murdered and that American Jews are connected to them. All Americans, except for Native Americans, have come at some point from somewhere abroad. For American Jews, the indelible images of the Holocaust have filled in that blurred vacancy with a sharply etched picture of the place they came from. If the knowledge of that place and its culture remains vague, at least the sense of loss and sadness elicited by the Holocaust has an address to which to attach itself.

Yet even for those who have been touched by "Holocaust consciousness," familiarity with the world of Eastern European Jewry rarely extends beyond a fascination with the liquidation of that world during the twelve years of the Third Reich. Whether the frame of reference is as large as the totality of Ashkenaz, the thousand years of Jewish creativity in Europe, or as narrow as the rise of Yiddish literature since the end of the nineteenth century, the years of the Nazi cataclysm are few and unrepresentative. Therefore, to allow, however unwittingly, the manner of the Jews' death to stand for or even epitomize the long line of this culture is not only to commit a historical untruth but also to betray the victims' conception of their own lives. It further skews our understanding by leading us to view the lives of East European Jews as if they were always being lived under the sign of extermination. This disproportion has very practical consequences. Universities are offered chairs of Holocaust Studies, but there are only sparse resources for the study of East European Jewish history; there seems to be an unlimited market for memoirs and books about the Holocaust but little interest in materials documenting the rich and varied life of the society that the Holocaust destroyed. The harshest critics of Holocaust centeredness do not put a fine point on it. What the Holocaust destroyed was awful enough, they argue, without our complicity in allowing it to become a kind of black hole that sucks in all the achievements of East European Jewry in the centuries that preceded it.

Fourth, for American Zionists the growing focus on the Holocaust has had a similar dual valence. Despite the considerable complexities of historical causation, the Holocaust and the establishment of the state of Israel have long and widely been inextricably linked in the popular mind. From the Eichmann trial forward Israel has cast itself in a vindicatory role in relationship to world Jewry vis-à-vis the Holocaust. Prime Minister Menachem Begin made the Holocaust a prominent theme in the political rhetoric through which he presented Israel to the world. The Holocaust has more recently become a tool in the hands of fund-raisers for increasing commitment to Israel through "missions" that first visit the concentration camps in Poland and then proceed to the homeland of the Jewish people in Israel.

The problem for Zionists involves a kind of role reversal. In contrast to—and in some ways because of—its relative silence during the Holocaust period, American Jewry was active on many levels on behalf of the creation of Israel and the interests of the young state through the fifties and sixties. American Jewish organizations and movements that had opposed Zionism or stood aloof from it shifted their stance toward support for the Jewish state in its struggle against its enemies. The sense of emergency on the eve of the Six-Day War and the victory that followed it electrified American Jews and opened up new avenues of connection with Israel and participation in its fortunes. In the seventies and eighties, however, when Israel became a less romantic and heroic object of identification for American Jews, the intensity of this engagement waned and the Holocaust presented itself as the up-and-coming cause in Jewish public life. The enormous energies—and resources—necessary to erect the museums and monuments came in part from American Jews who had been active in other Jewish causes, especially those related to Israel, and in part from those whose consciences and imaginations were touched by the Holocaust in ways they had not been by other Jewish causes.

Finally, conscience is not the only source of this moral power, argue the critics of Holocaust centeredness. In *The Holocaust in*

The Future of Memorialization

American Life, Peter Novick points to what he calls the politics of victimization as a stronger explanation.[2] The base of political and moral authority of different groups in American society shifted during this period from collective achievement to collective deprivation. Rather than pointing to what its members had accomplished in America, groups identified themselves instead with the historical sufferings—slavery, discrimination, internment—to which they had been subjected. According to these new criteria, American Jews gained little from the fact that they had overcome immigrant poverty and anti-Semitism and that Israel, with which American Jews were closely identified, had succeeded in becoming a regional power in the Middle East. Their very success placed American Jews on the side of the oppressors and the majority culture. Yet when it came to historical suffering, the Jews did in fact have a calamity to offer that could tie if not trump the claims of other groups. The enormity of the Holocaust, and the moral claims that issued from it, were uncontestable to all but those on the farthest fringes of society. As coreligionists of the Six Million, as Novick has contentiously observed, American Jews were "intent on permanent possession of the gold medal in the Victimization Olympics."[3]

Do these critiques, taken together, persuade us that American Jews are in fact overly preoccupied with the Holocaust? Yes and no. When interest in the Holocaust crowds out knowledge and appreciation of the larger enterprise of Jewish civilization, then there is indeed warrant to see a troubling disproportion. This is certainly the case in the eyes of groups and movements within the American Jewish community that are trying to advance what they regard as a positive and substantive vision of Judaism as a way of life. The Holocaust deserves to be elaborately commemorated as a central event in modern Jewish experience, they would readily concede, but it does not—and should not—constitute either a way of life or the primary foundation for a viable Jewish identity. This holds true not only for the synagogue movements, which advocate comprehensive programs of ritual observance, text study, and social action, but also for groups

The Future of Memorialization

that work to strengthen the ties of American Jews to Israel and to the culture of Eastern Europe. The charge of exploiting the Holocaust has generally been laid at the doorstep of what are called the Jewish defense organizations, especially the Anti-Defamation League. Through mass mailings and media presentations, it is argued, these groups have seized upon the sensationalism of the Holocaust to shake American Jews free of their complacency, keep them vigilant and insecure (despite the widespread retreat of anti-Semitism in the post-war period), and thus keep these organizations alive.[4]

Whether this charge can be sustained is beside the main point: Many American Jews are in fact alive to the message being broadcast at them and find in the Holocaust a special point of interest. For how many it becomes a point of active involvement or commitment is hard to say. It is in general exceptionally difficult to map the distribution of this interest, and to say, for example, that it forms a substitute identity for Jews who lack substantive religious affiliations or, alternatively, that it functions as a supplement for those who already have strong communal involvements. It would be instructive to know, for instance, who are the purchasers and readers of the hundreds of books published yearly concerning the Holocaust. It would be similarly instructive to discover whether the individuals who have been active in organizing and funding the various museums and memorials are active in other Jewish communal affairs and institutions or whether their Holocaust involvement stands alone. We would benefit from understanding the motives of Jewish students enrolled in the numerous courses on the Holocaust taught on college campuses. There are numbers of other measures that would bring us some clarity about this phenomenon. Yet I know of no survey research yet available that would satisfy this curiosity, so we are left for the time being to our surmises and anecdotal observations.

Whether it serves as a stand-alone identity or as an add-on, identification with the Holocaust undeniably plays a role in the lives of American Jews. If communal organizations are sometimes opportunistic in their use of the Holocaust, there is less reason to think this is the case when it comes to lives of individuals. It has been a recurrent question in this book why gentile America should care about a calamity that happened far away and long ago. But the fact that American Jews care about the Holocaust should in no way be taken for granted. For American Jews the event is also distant, and the intervening effects of Americanization have been staggering. Some of the cultural and political developments that led American Jews as a group, despite their aloofness, to forge a connection with the fate of European Jewry were surveyed in chapter 1. There is a factor that needs to be added now because it sheds light on the motivations of American Jews as individuals rather than as members of a corporate entity.

This is a factor that I will call, borrowing a phrase from novelist Norma Rosen, touching evil.[5] Most American Jews who came of age after the war grew up under conditions of physical safety and material sufficiency. This was not, to be sure, a life in which suffering was unknown. Children were born with crippling diseases or died in accidents; grown-ups contracted cancer, or died young of heart attacks, or suffered mental breakdowns; businesses failed and infidelities broke up families. Yet none of these calamities, as awful as they were for those affected, subverted the essential conviction of civil order under which Jews lived. When American Jews eventually "discovered" the Holocaust, or more accurately, had the Holocaust placed before them by all of the cultural mediations discussed earlier on, they discovered evil and suffering that were at once utterly foreign and utterly familiar. The unspeakable crimes perpetrated by the Nazis strained the American moral imagination, yet the victims of these crimes had been the brothers and sisters of American Jews, who, even if they had long distanced themselves from their European coreligionists, had nonetheless never renounced their fundamental filiation.

For the bystander American Jew, the slaughtered European Jew became a kind of doppelganger, or double; and the Nazi perpetrators became figures of a monstrous, shadow evil. To see the pictures

The Future of Memorialization

and to read the accounts meant to touch this evil—even if it were through the heavy folds of an invisible and vicarious veil. There was the awful frisson of identifying with the fate of European Jewry, crossing the distance from here to there, touching events of life and death—and all this without the exposure to genuine danger. Now, by noting this fascination and vicarious experience, it is far from my intention to label it as bad faith or to expose it as a cheap psychological mechanism. To the contrary, I take this impulse on the part of American Jews as the sign of a deep and authentic desire to reach beyond the conditions imposed upon them by the American milieu and their attenuated relationship to history. For some, of course, the fascination may be morbid and even prurient, and for others the form it takes may be disfigured by obsession or aggression. Yet for many, engagement with the Holocaust should be taken as a symptom of something more positive: an implicit awareness on the part of American Jews of how very insulated their lives have been from the turbulent currents of modern Jewish history.

I count myself in this last category. My grandparents came to the United States from Lithuania in the 1880s, and by the time I was growing up there was no longer any contact with family that had stayed in Europe. I knew no survivors in my community except for one Hebrew school teacher, or for that matter any Jews who were not American born. The suburban synagogue culture in which I was raised during the fifties and sixties placed a premium on ritual observance and a knowledge of Hebrew language and culture. My involvements in Jewish youth movements and Jewish summer camping strengthened and extended my understanding of Judaism as a system of symbols, values, and experiences. This was a conception that, except for an admiration for Israel, had little to do with the violent transformations of Jewish life in Europe and Russia. My interest in the Holocaust, which was informal and unrelated to my professional studies, began when I was a graduate student in the seventies. In retrospect I understand the impetus for this interest to have come from the kind of awareness of insufficiency I described above. I recognized that the Judaism I possessed was a sensitive plant that flourished on the soil of the Diaspora, well protected from transformative and catastrophic events that had swept through and swept away the lives of much of world Jewry during my century. I am sure that I did not want to renounce my protectedness, but I did seek at least to touch the violent core of these events by knowing as much about them as I could and by opening my mind to the difficult theological challenges they posed. The murder of European Jewry thus came to serve as a reference point of ultimate gravity. While my Jewish practice and commitments were not greatly altered, they came to be framed by that awful event. Through reference to the Holocaust I became more conscious of the particularly American nature of the Jewish identity I had constructed.

It is perfectly clear that in so doing I was "using" the Holocaust for purposes that only in part stemmed from the Holocaust itself. I have pointed to my own case not in order to offer an apologia for myself but to present an illustration of the fact that engagement with the Holocaust is always mixed up with ulterior motives. This is not a truth that is unique to the Holocaust. Any kind of altruistic or idealistic commitment, whether to political movements, religion, or social welfare, is invariably a tangled knot of personal needs and larger ideals. Most such commitments are initiated through socialization and inculcation or are precipitated by personal exigency or self-interest. In the best of cases, through knowledge and self-reflection, the balance shifts over time toward a greater allegiance to the ideals and practices themselves, although the complicit complexity of the mixture of motivations will never be dissolved.

Interest and involvement in Holocaust memory is not precisely analogous to the practice of a religious faith or devotion to a political program, but the resemblances are clear enough. There are a variety of actions an American Jew might undertake to express this interest: contributing time or money or political influence to the creation of Holocaust museums and memorials, buying and reading memoirs and works of history, viewing films and television programs on the subject, attending lectures and seasonal memorial gatherings and ceremonies, traveling to the sites of slaughter in Europe and to memorials in Israel. As manifold as these expressions of interest are, the accompanying motives have little to do with the intrinsic enterprise of Holocaust memory: desire for social prominence, the moral prestige that attaches to the status of ultimate victims, a mode of connection with the Jewish community that bypasses religion and Israel, a historical analogy that strengthens Israel's leverage in international relations, a desire to touch the turbulence of modern Jewish history (as described above), survivor guilt and an identification with the victims, and various forms of religious duty. This inventory could be augmented and elaborated, but the point would be the same. For American Jews, activity on behalf of Holocaust memory is inextricably wrapped around a set of extrinsic needs and interests.

Now a moralist might rate these motives along a scale that ranges from the "pure" to the "impure" and judge a person on where he or she stood between these poles. Yet, as I have argued, the situation is no different from what we find when we probe the motives for religious observance, altruistic behavior, and political commitment. There is no more reason to expect purity here than in the case of the Holocaust. Furthermore, just as we accept the value of acts of piety and self-sacrifice as end products despite the mixture of their motives, by the same score we need not deny the legitimacy of acts of Holocaust remembrance whose provenance is similarly compromised.

THE DYNAMICS OF MEMORIALIZATION

What we do have a right to expect, however, is a degree of self-awareness. This is an awareness that swings in two directions: the current complexity of motivations and the future modes of memorialization. In order to turn toward the challenge of the future, in which the question of intentionality will be paramount, I wish to

The Future of Memorialization

shift the discussion from American Jews to all Americans and from the behavior of the individual to the life of communities. For if the situation of American Jews is complicated, then how much more so is the situation of American *non*-Jews, whose relationship to the Holocaust is rooted in no obvious ethnic or religious kinship? What does it mean for African-Americans, Native Americans, and Armenian-Americans—each group with its historical calamity— to remember the murder of European Jewry? Surely the reasons believing Christians take part in Holocaust memorialization must likewise be layered and multiple.

We are desperately in need of a way to understand this daunting complexity. Yet the model we now have at our disposal is a rigid rhetoric of purity and impurity that compounds the difficulty. There are those who use and abuse the Holocaust and those who remain loyal to its true import; and, unsurprisingly, the former is usually the other and the latter the self. We construct an ideal of authenticity and are quick to identify betrayals and exploitations. There are those who "get it right" and those who enlist this great tragedy to further other agendas. The result is a contentious politics of blame and self-righteousness rather than a broadening cultural dialectic. The perpetuation of Holocaust memory is hardly served thereby. For this state of contention further detracts from the greatest challenge facing us in the future: preserving Holocaust memory in the absence of witnesses and in a society in which the pendulum of attention is just as likely to swing away from the Holocaust as it has recently swung toward it.

I would propose an alternative model that sees the meaning of the Holocaust as being constructed by overlapping communities of interpretation in American society. This approach harks back to the constructivist premise that was explored in chapter 2. The assumption is that beyond its factual core the meaning of the Holocaust, like all historical events, is not inscribed in the event itself but shaped by interpreters that come after it. What bears emphasis at this juncture is the collective dimension of this meaning-giving activity.

The Future of Memorialization

Despite the infinite varieties of individual temperament and personal history, the most productive way to understand the shaping of Holocaust memory in America is to look at the interpretive communities from within which individuals understand the world around them.

I take the term *interpretive community* from the discourse of literary theory.[6] The term was developed as a way to mediate between subjectivism and the presumption of objective meaning. On the one hand, a literary text can be taken to have as many meanings as readers, each reader construing the text in his or her idiosyncratic way. On the other hand, the text can be taken to have a discoverable intrinsic meaning that is guaranteed by the author's intention or by the cultural norms of the period in which it was written. The notion of the interpretive community stakes out a median position between the two, and it does so not simply as a standard of common sense but out of the conviction that meaning is a social product. We live in communities of shared values and outlooks that differentiate us from other communities, and it is from within these networks that we understand the world around us and its cultural artifacts. While we may reject the assertion that a text can mean only one thing, we also know that it cannot mean anything; and the field of possibility that remains is bounded by the affinity we feel with the minds and values of other interpreters.

The application to the shaping of Holocaust memory in America is evident: different groups (interpretive communities) have construed the Holocaust differently over the past fifty years and will continue to play a defining role in the future. The term *group*, or *interpretive community*, in the American context is admittedly protean and even vague but, I believe, unavoidably so. There is little purpose in speaking of African-Americans as a group or Jews as a group or Christians as a group. We have seen that American Jewry, which forms a tiny minority within the American polity, contains within it a number of different communities, which have in turn taken different stances toward the "message" of the Holocaust. These groups are sometimes overlapping within the larger Jewish community and almost always overlapping with circles in general American culture; and individual Jews will often maintain multiple memberships and be influenced by multiple perspectives. The intensity of these distinctions among American Jews is of course the result of the intensity of proprietary feelings toward the Holocaust. Yet distinctions abound—if perhaps less charged and reticulated—in attitudes toward the Holocaust on the part of the vast majority of the American population that is not Jewish.

Despite all of this multiplicity, the notion of the group or the interpretive community remains centrally useful to an analysis of the reception of the Holocaust in America. The meaning given the Holocaust at different points in the past is largely a function of the needs and interests of these different groups. For example, when it comes to covering the Holocaust period, Jewish history textbooks used in the schools of the Reform and Conservative movements in American Judaism during the fifties stress the Warsaw ghetto uprising, acts of individual resistance, and the participation of Jewish GIs in the American war effort.[7] This incorporation of the Holocaust into a heroic tradition should be seen as a reflection of the contemporaneous needs of these groups: a desire to participate in an optimistic postwar outlook and not to stand apart from the American nation, a concomitant reluctance to be identified with the victims of persecution, and a strong connection to Israel's struggle for independence and security.

As a contrastive example, we can adduce again the March of the Living, the program that takes teenagers on a very concentrated pilgrimage first to the concentration camps in Poland and then to Israel. The trip began in the eighties under the sponsorship of Jewish communal agencies in Israel and America outside the framework of the synagogue movements. This frontal exposure to the sites of slaughter answers to a different set of concerns that arose from an acute anxiety about Jewish "continuity." As a term in wide use in communal discourse at the time, Jewish continuity was the rather

The Future of Memorialization

euphemistic name associated with American Jewry's great nightmare: that it would wither away and disappear through high rates of inter-marriage and extreme acculturation. The Holocaust, as evoked by the physical remainders of the concentration camps and by a shocking exposure to Jewish victimization, was deemed the only "Jewish" experience with the emotional impact necessary to pierce this alien-ation and regenerate a connection to the Jewish people that would be at least sufficient to prevent Jews from marrying non-Jews.

Now in both of these cases, taken from different circles within the Jewish community and separated by three decades, the Holocaust is interpreted differently in order to reinforce different sets of val-ues. This does not mean, it should be stressed again, that one appro-priation is more sincere than the other or that either is insincere in the desire to memorialize the Holocaust. It means simply—though in another sense this use is never simple at all—that different inter-pretive communities will construe the event in different ways.

But what of the future? It is not difficult, I think, to apply this rubric profitably to the many efforts at Holocaust memorialization that abound in American life today as well as to those that were mounted in the past. It is a greater challenge to think about the future. Because of the hushed reverence with which the Holocaust is gen-erally treated, few groups presume to think instrumentally about the role they wish it to play in the future development of their institu-tions. There are, to be sure, some strident voices with clear politi-cal motives that have their slogans already in place. But most groups are stumbling along into the future under the cover of convenient mystifications about the Holocaust and complacently vague banal-ities about the imperative never to forget. This unconsciousness will not be put to the test under the conditions that presently obtain in America: the museums, the books, the videos, and the high degree of moral prestige given to a Jewish tragedy by the general society. Yet those conditions will change and have already begun to do so. When the widespread acceptability of the Holocaust wanes, it will behoove us—and by *us* I mean the multiplicity of communities that

The Future of Memorialization

make up America—to have given thoughtful consideration to ways in which we want to remember the Holocaust and have that memory make a creative and constructive contribution to our values and goals.

To make what is at stake more concrete I present the following thought experiment. Let us imagine four high schools' trips to visit the U.S. Holocaust Memorial Museum in Washington, D.C. One school is a public high school in the Midwest whose students come primarily from Lutheran backgrounds; another is a Roman Catholic parochial school in the inner city; another is a Modern Orthodox Jewish day school; and the last is a youth group of a suburban synagogue whose members attend the local public high school. Let us further think of ourselves as the educators who are preparing the students for the trip, helping them to frame their experience while at the museum, and integrate it once they have returned home.

The educators planning the trip of the Midwestern students are likely to present the Holocaust as an aspect of the American experience of World War II: the genocidal atrocities as an example of the Nazi menace Americans fought against and defeated. For this view there will be ample evidence in the museum. The educators will try to prepare the students for the shock of the sights they will see, which will be understood as the worst manifestations of inhumanity along a gradient of other twentieth-century mass crimes. As for the Jews as Jews, the educators will be in something of a dilemma. Their students are likely never to have met Jews or observed Jewish life. The vivid images of Jews they will meet in the museum—the urban Jews, East and West, dressed in suits and hats, the village Jews with beards and side curls, the emaciated and dehumanized visages of the camp inmates—will mark the Jews in their mind as tragic, pitiable, and alien. The connection between these ghostly images and the actuality of American Jewry or, for that matter, Israeli Jewry, will be difficult to establish, and the gap will likely remain wide.

In the case of the students from the Catholic inner-city school, there is likely to be a similar framing of the Holocaust within the

American experience of World War II. Yet because most of the students are African-American and Hispanic, the educators planning the trip will also address the analogies between the murder of Europe's Jews and the institution of chattel slavery and the colonial genocides committed against aboriginal peoples. The persistence of the Holocaust in the minds of these students in the future will largely depend on the strength of these analogies. The educators might also hope that the pathos elicited by the graphic depictions of the Jews' fate will humanize their students' perceptions of Jews, who probably now appear to the students only as members of a particularly successful white ethnic group. The Catholic dimension of the school might lead educators to anticipate questions concerning the role of the church during the Holocaust and to stress the instances of the rescue of Jews by individual Catholics and whole communities. The Pope's recent teachings about religious tolerance and the Jews might be presented as a larger framework for understanding the theological status of the Jewish victims and surviving world Jewry; yet it should not be taken for granted that the students will be informed about the darker side of the historical relations between the church and the Jews.

The situation of the students from the Modern Orthodox Jewish day school will be different from all the others in the amount of information and "Holocaust consciousness" they will likely already have in hand. They will have grown up hearing innumerable anecdotes, attending solemn assemblies, and interacting with survivors and their descendents in everyday life. In their worldview, the Holocaust will likely have been construed as the latest and most tragic chapter in the millennial persecution of the Jews by the gentile nations and as directly linked to a fierce commitment to the defense of Israel. The challenge to the educators orienting the students for the trip will be to prepare them for the American narrative with its universalist implications told by the Washington museum. Whether the Holocaust and its message can be "shared" with other Americans will be an issue to be contended with. Even within the parochial context of Jewish remembrance, there will be much discussion as to whether the Holocaust should stand alone in its own commemorative space—with the suggestion of its unresolved theological uniqueness—or whether it should be absorbed into the paradigm of the destruction of the Jerusalem Temple and the hallowed traditions of Jewish mourning.

Finally, the suburban synagogue youth-group members can be counted on to have some familiarity with the Holocaust, but because their Jewish schooling has been spotty and inconsistent, they will have a poor grasp of Jewish history and practice as a framework for understanding the murder of European Jewry. It is just this slender purchase on Jewish knowledge and commitment that is likely to weigh on the minds of the trip's planners. They see the hearts and minds of their young people being won by the memory-less consumer culture that surrounds them, and they are afraid that the ethnic and family bonds that still bind will not long prevent marriages to non-Jews. The Holocaust represents a kind of last chance to shock their young charges out of their complacency, establish an empathic connection with the victims of anti-Semitism, and lead them to an identification with the distinctiveness of Jewish fate—and all this for the greater purpose of eventually making them into active members of the American Jewish community.

I have purposefully chosen to frame this exercise from the educators' point of view because it is relatively easy for us to identify with a sense of professional and moral responsibility for guiding the steps of young people. It is much more difficult for us to take responsibility for *ourselves*. The discussion of educational goals undertaken separately but in parallel by these four groups in preparation for their Washington trip is intended to serve as a figure for the kind of deliberative processes that should be taking place in many quarters in America. Rather than being polite and making pious gestures toward the sanctity of the Holocaust or rather than attacking the vulgarizations of the Holocaust in American culture, it is imperative, in my view, for various groups in America to think purposefully about the claims made upon them by the Holocaust and, in turn, about how Holocaust memory contributes to the construction of their future visions. I find it astonishing that two of the major synagogue movements on the American scene, Reform and Conservative Judaism, have declined to designate this as a task for serious thought and policy making. As a result they have been moved to the margins by the enormous engine of memorialization activity and have lost the chance to shape this energy according to their own lights and even to make use of it to advance the larger aims of their movements.

Let there be many visions, and let them converse with one another and present attractive and persuasive arguments for their positions. But let no group, not even survivors, claim that only they guard the sanctity of Holocaust memory and only their motives are free from taint. For if the purity of Holocaust memory is cordoned off and protected—which I believe is impossible to begin with—and if it is *not* admixed with other values and aspirations, then it will wither to the point of becoming little more than a museum artifact.

VIDEOTAPED SURVIVOR TESTIMONY AS THE NEW ARCHIVE OF THE HOLOCAUST

As the visions of Holocaust memory in America are being constructed, the exigent question will become what they should be constructed of. What are the resources and materials that can be utilized to make these visions—however much they differ one from the other—palpable, affecting, and persuasive? Scholarship will continue to contribute new perspectives; films, novels, plays, music, visual art, and poetry will make their contribution; museums will go on displaying artifacts and mounting exhibits. But the most visible and popularly disseminated resource will be a new one: survivor testimony recorded on videotape. The largest undertaking by far to record and catalog survivor testimony has been initiated by Steven Spielberg through his Survivors of the Shoah Visual History Foundation.

The Future of Memorialization

The story of this project is a quintessentially American tale, and as a conclusion to this study of the Americanization of the Holocaust, no more emblematic an instance could be adduced. The making of his Holocaust film, as we have seen, coincided with Spielberg's active return to his Jewish roots, his recommitment to fatherhood and family, and the deployment of his mastery of film technique for serious purposes. Beseeched by survivors who were not Schindler Jews to tell their stories as well, Spielberg laid the groundwork for a vast effort to locate survivors, videotape their testimony, and make it available for posterity. It was a race against time because the survivors were dying off. The foundation Spielberg created hastened to assemble production crews, train interviewers, and fan out across America at first and then on to Israel, South America, the former Soviet Union, and anywhere else in the world where there remained survivors to tell their story. By the end of 1998, only four years after the inception of the project, no fewer than fifty thousand testimonies had been recorded.

It was not just an organizational feat. Spielberg saw in the innovations of technology a way to forestall the fading of memory. While the very existence of inexpensive videography was the first step, digitization became the new frontier. The taped testimony was sent in from all over the world to the project's headquarters in a series of trailers on the back lot of Universal Studios in Hollywood. There the tapes were copied and transferred to digital format and handed over to catalogers. In around-the-clock shifts, the catalogers now sit before computer monitors and, using specially designed software, break down each testimony into several-minute sections, make note of the content, and cross-reference it according to a lexicon of over ten thousand keywords. Years from now—no one knows exactly how many years—when the vast task of cataloging is finally completed, it will be possible for historians and educators to search this immense archive for specific information, and they will be referred not to whole, several-hour testimonies but to precise segments relevant to the query. If advances in the storage and transmission of electronic

The Future of Memorialization

data accelerate, the resources of the archive would be accessible to all from remote locations via the Internet. Until such time as this vision is realized, the foundation will take evocative pieces of testimony and make them available to the public in various combinations and packages as documentary films and CDs.

This is, by any account, an extraordinary achievement. It is at the same time a flawed achievement. The Spielberg project ignored the valuable experience with video testimony that had earlier been accumulated by others and gave little thought to how the testimony might eventually be used. Scant use was made of historians in conceiving of and carrying out the project. The greatest problem was the lack of training of the army of volunteer interviewers mobilized for the task. While some were knowledgeable about the Holocaust and Jewish life in Europe, many were not, and to compensate for this variability the interviewers were given uniform protocols that fit the testimony into set time blocks (a formula for the amount of time to be devoted to life before the war, the war years themselves, and to life afterward). A softening and harmonizing of memory were encouraged by conducting the interviews in the survivor's home and by inviting the survivor's family to join him or her in the final moments of the taping session. Finally, from now until the cataloging is finished, which may be a very long time indeed, the foundation allows no access to the testimony it has gathered, and the in-house documentaries and educational materials produced so far have been slick and mediocre.

In the renowned tradition of American philanthropy, Steven Spielberg has given a great deal, but he has given on his own terms. He has given a great deal of money, and he has used his fame and his power to draw national attention to the Holocaust and the need to remember it. At the same time, he has put the indelible stamp of Hollywood production values upon the endeavor and displayed a prodigious degree of anti-intellectualism in building his project from the ground up without regard for previous achievements. It is a larger-than-life story in every respect, and we are put in the

The Future of Memorialization

position of having to be grateful for a beneficence that has been visited upon us. Although the archive will undoubtedly be a substantial achievement, it is not easy to forget how much better it could have been.

The wisdom that was put aside came from the Fortunoff Video Archive at Yale University, which began recording survivor testimonies in 1979 and had recorded forty-four hundred testimonies as of 1999. The model developed by the Yale project was different in several respects. The interviews were conducted by a small group of volunteers (among them a significant proportion of psychologists and academics) who built up a considerable store of knowledge about the historical circumstances of the Holocaust and each of whom stayed with the project for a number of years. The Yale interviewers strove to structure the session with the survivor as little as possible. Rather than proceeding from a set of protocols, they intervened only to clarify, aiming instead to create a neutral field that would allow the survivors to tell their stories in any kind of chronological, associative, or digressive manner they wished. The sessions were allowed to go on for as long as the survivor wished to speak, and some lasted more than a day. Although the tapes are not digitized, there is a detailed cataloging system, which is available on the Internet, and each testimony is accompanied by an extensive set of notes with numerical time markings taken by the interviewer that allow the viewer to go directly to a specific subject. The tapes are accessible to all, although the sign-in procedures and the hushed quiet of the Manuscripts and Archives reading room at Sterling Memorial Library make it clear that this is not a setting for casual use.

Yet even if the lessons of the Yale archive had been integrated by the Spielberg project—and it is clear that some of them would not have worked in an all-out campaign to gather tens of thousands of testimonies in a few years—there still remain serious impediments to the use of video testimony altogether, whether it emanates from Los Angeles or New Haven. Amid the celebration of the medium and its role in rescuing survivor testimony, we need to be cognizant

The Future of Memorialization

of the challenges presented by this format and the problems we will have to solve in order to make use of its potential value.

The greatest issue is the nearly unchartable vastness of the material. As of the summer of 1999, the Shoah Foundation reported that it had collected 116,593 hours of testimony. If a viewer watched eight hours a day five days a week, it would take fifty-six years to view the entire archive. Now of course there will be indexes and computerized searches that will purportedly help navigation within the archive. For certain types of focused historical inquiries the collection will undoubtedly be a very promising resource. A historian will theoretically be able to delimit a search, say to female children in hiding in Government Poland or to the events in a particular camp during a particular month, push a button, and obtain relevant references to several-minute segments from the testimonies of many different survivors and, depending on the technology available at the time, either request the individual tapes from a central repository or see them immediately on a monitor.

Yet if the object of research is psychological, theological, or literary in nature, it will not be so easy to frame an inquiry that brings useful results. Take for example Lawrence Langer's eloquent study *Holocaust Testimonies: The Ruins of Memory*, in which he uses the tapes in the Yale archive to delineate different types of Holocaust memory and how that memory erupts into the present life of the survivor. Langer based his analysis on hundreds, perhaps thousands, of hours of testimonies he viewed from beginning to end, many of which he knew intimately because he himself was the interviewer or he knew about them from consultations among the close circle of interviewers at the Yale project. Given the kind of cathartic moments and narrative breakthroughs he was searching for, it is doubtful whether he would have benefited greatly from brief cross-referenced segments of testimony. If I were to write a book about survivor testimonies, I would be interested in looking for something quite different from Langer's subject. I would want to research the issue of continuity and reconstruction in the lives of survivors rather than the debilitating effects of memory. But I would be at a loss as to how to proceed, where to start, where to dip in; and I cannot conceive of being hugely aided by some elegant Boolean search and the neat snippets of testimony it would offer me. Because of his devotion and participation, Langer was already enviably located, as it were, inside the archive. I see myself standing outside without a clue as to which door to knock on.

The great point about the use of the archive of Holocaust video testimony is that our contact with it will always have to be mediated. There will be those happy few who acquire the necessary skills and whose questions will be satisfied by narrowly focused factual searches. For most Americans, however, the contribution to Holocaust memory made by these archives in the future—not to mention the indefinite present during which the Spielberg archive is neither accessible nor searchable—will come from preselected anthologies of edited testimony. Examples of such projects include *The Last Days*, *The Lost Children of Berlin*, and *Survivors of the Holocaust*, all documentary films produced by the survivors of the Shoah Foundation and based on their collected testimonies. The Fortunoff Video Archive offers schools a selection of edited testimonies, some by individuals and some put together in thematic groups. On can admire the selecting and editing of testimony and the production values of some of these products more than others, but in the end one cannot argue with their inevitability. We will necessarily always be beholden to a class of Holocaust educator-archivists—I don't know what else to call them—who, selecting and editing and splicing, will act as a kind of interface between the oceanic variety of the archive and our own wonderment.

Will we be in good hands? I am not sanguine. Interpreters, first of all, need to be possessed of a familiarity with the way of life of the victims before the war in all its geographical and cultural diversity and with the intimate language and unnatural society of the ghettos, concentration camps, and DP camps. But even if this knowledge is acquired, and it can be, there remains the unmapped difficulty of

The Future of Memorialization

the oral testimony itself. We have not yet learned how to read and interpret Holocaust testimonies critically; and by critically I do not mean judgmentally but with the ability to locate and describe a given testimony within a set of categories and concepts. For example, anyone who has viewed a sampling of these testimonies is struck by the fact that nearly every survivor avers that he or she had a very happy childhood and was raised within a loving family. At the same time, we know that these years were a period of economic depression, political turmoil, and rapid secularization and urbanization and that the resulting pressures upon families were enormous. In a similar vein, most survivors direct their rage against the Nazi perpetrators and their local proxies and speak little about collaborators and the deceitful behavior of fellow Jews. Here too we know from the historical record and contemporaneous testimony that such behavior was rife and the object of deep and implacable hatred on the part of Jews who were its victims. Now, it goes without saying that these denials have nothing to do with concealment and everything to do with the way in which memory shapes itself fifty years after an event. It is just these sorts of transformational principles operating within Holocaust testimonies that need to be described and made part of critical awareness in approaching these materials.

We still have a great deal to learn about how these testimonies work. Each testimony may indeed be—or at least be experienced by the survivor as—a naive, authentic, and original account of a particular individual's experience, while at the same time being governed by a variety of models whose normative power the survivor has little awareness of. Witnesses intuit models for what a proper survivor narrative should be and often adapt the raw material of their experience to this armature. This is a process that only strengthens over the decades as survivors share stories with each other, read memoirs, and repeat their memories before audiences in need of certain kinds of nourishment and stimulation. Different master narratives emerge, and some have greater force than others, such as the death-in-life narrative implicit in Wiesel's *Night*, as was discussed in chap-

The Future of Memorialization

ter 2. These, again, are precisely the kind of categories that have to be laid out to form part of a map of critical understanding. It is only with this map in hand that the uniqueness of an individual testimony can be given its due and truly appreciated. This is the kind of critical awareness that, once it is developed, will have to form part of the essential repertoire of skills possessed by the educator-archivists who will descend into the sea of testimony so that they can show us how to navigate our way.

A final consideration bears on the relative authority of video testimony. The survivors have suffered much and have born witness as a gift to future generations, and we accept the gift and deeply honor their experience. Is it therefore disrespectful to state that the historical value of their testimony is less than—or at least qualified in relationship to—other forms of witness that have been less sought after and celebrated? We have already called attention to the corpus of the Ringelblum archive that lies inert in Warsaw, perhaps to be published in Polish but not in English. There is an additional body of material that is more closely twinned to the archive of video testimony now being consolidated in America. I refer to the thousands of pages of written testimony held by the Yad Vashem Holocaust Memorial Authority in Jerusalem. These are eyewitness accounts recorded by survivors in the immediate aftermath of the war in the several languages that the survivors spoke. They are raw, angry, and anguished; they are not written from the retrospective point of view of reconstituted family lives and successful businesses, and they do not turn away in silence from the acts of treachery Jews committed against Jews. This body of material is also troped and shaped according to narrative models and needs to be mapped and understood critically.

Yet unless there is some sudden change in circumstance, this material, despite its manifest value on many levels, is not going to be translated, digitized, and rendered searchable and packaged for the classroom. Perhaps one day a philanthropist such as Steven Spielberg or the considerable research resources of the U.S. Holocaust

The Future of Memorialization

Memorial Museum will make the recovery of these materials possible. In the meantime, while we celebrate the unprecedented gathering of video testimony, it is important to acknowledge the relative position of the American project in a context framed by the unpublished Ringelblum archive, documents of other ghettos, and the survivor accounts at Yad Vashem and other repositories.

We live in an age in which the Great Archive of the Holocaust is being established. It will encompass the testimonies of the survivors and the documents of the ghettos; the museums and the memorials; the assiduous research of historians, psychologists, and literary critics; the thoughts of philosophers and theologians; the artistic responses of writers, painters, musicians, and liturgists; and, of course, the artifacts of popular culture. Even after the broad public fascination with the Holocaust wanes, the Archive will stand and, one hopes, be augmented by future generations.

There are two ways to enter the Archive. One can enter at random, touching what is closest at hand and, in turn, being touched by it. But the Archive will open itself most abundantly and revealingly to those who come with questions in hand; and each of the communities of America, in its struggle to give creative shape to the memory of the Holocaust, will approach with a different set of queries. It is formulating the questions that will be the hard part.

Notes

1. Peter Novick's *The Holocaust in American Life* (Boston: Houghton Mifflin, 1999), which reached me after the burden of my argument was framed, is an ambitious attempt to offer a similar account of how the Holocaust became prominent in American society. The book's most valuable sections, to my mind, deal with the forties and fifties and the role of the Cold War in shaping American perceptions of the recent past. As the volume's focus moves toward the present, however, its argument becomes more tendentious and is marked by a lack of empathy for its subject. Despite Novick's enormous erudition, he gives short shrift to the role of popular culture in making the Holocaust an American concern rather than just a Jewish one. See also the perceptive essay by Alvin Rosenfeld, *The Americanization of the Holocaust,* David W. Belin Lecture in American Jewish Affairs (Ann Arbor: University of Michigan, 1995), and the essays collected in Hilene Flanzbaum, ed., *The Americanization of the Holocaust* (Baltimore: Johns Hopkins University Press, 1999).

2. Two balanced studies of the war years and their immediate aftermath are Deborah E. Lipstadt, *The American Press and the Coming of the Holocaust, 1933–1945* (New York: Free Press, 1986), and Henry L. Feingold, *Bearing Witness: How America and Its Jews Responded to the Holocaust* (Syracuse, N.Y.: Syracuse University Press, 1995).

3. I am admittedly filling in this story with very broad strokes. There is much work to be done in fleshing out our picture of the late forties and the fifties. Awareness of the Holocaust can be found in some fiction and reportage, both directly and in displaced form. The work of David G. Myers

Notes

promises to be illuminating in this regard. See his "Responsible for Every Single Pain: Holocaust Literature and the Ethics of Interpretation," *Comparative Literature* 51 (fall 1999). A good example of this close attention is the more-than-expected treatment of the Holocaust in the serious live dramas aired on national television during the fifties, as explored by Jeffrey Shandler in *While America Watches: Televising the Holocaust* (New York: Oxford University Press, 1999). Rona Sheramy has widened our knowledge by researching the curricula of Jewish schools during this period in "Defining Lessons: Holocaust Education and American Jewish Youth from World War II to the Present" (Ph.D. diss., Brandeis University, 2000).

4. For an expanded discussion of Israeli culture and the Holocaust, see my *ḤURBAN: Responses to Catastrophe in Hebrew Literature* (New York: Columbia University Press, 1984; Syracuse, N.Y.: Syracuse University Press, 1996). This subject was treated polemically by Tom Segev in *The Seventh Million: The Israelis and the Holocaust* (New York: Hill and Wang, 1995). For a more scholarly treatment of a major facet of the problem, see Dina Porat, *The Blue and the Yellow Stars of David: The Zionist Leadership in Palestine and the Holocaust, 1939–1945* (Cambridge: Harvard University Press, 1990).

5. See Novick, *Holocaust in American Life,* 189–203.

6. Jeffrey Shandler's study of the representation of the Holocaust on television is a pathbreaking work toward this end. Judith E. Doneson makes a signal contribution when it comes to the big screen in her *The Holocaust in American Film* (Philadelphia: Jewish Publication Society, 1987). Doneson's study includes a broad interpretation of the shifting attitudes of American Jews, which I found illuminating.

7. Two recent studies deal with this topic from contrastive points of view: Lawrence Graver, *An Obsession with Anne Frank* (Berkeley and Los Angeles: University of California Press, 1995) and Ralph Melnick, *The Stolen Legacy of Anne Frank: Meyer Levin, Lillian Hellman, and the Staging of the Diary* (New Haven, Conn.: Yale University Press, 1997). A careful and far-ranging analysis of the reception of the diary and the figure of Anne Frank is to be found in Alex Sagan, 'I want to go on living even after my death': The Popularization of Anne Frank and the Limits of Historical Consciousness" (Ph.D. diss., Harvard University, 1998) and "An Optimistic Icon: Anne Frank's Canonization in Postwar Culture," *German Politics and Society* 13, no. 3 (fall 1995).

8. This work was submitted for publication in 1954 and published in 1956 in Argentina. According to Wiesel in his *All Rivers Run to the Sea: Memoirs* (New York: Knopf, 1995), he edited the 862 pages of the manuscript into the 245 pages of the published Yiddish edition. *La Nuit* was 178

Notes

pages. For an illuminating comparison between the Yiddish and French versions, see Naomi Seidman, "Elie Wiesel and the Scandal of Jewish Rage," *Jewish Social Studies* (New Series) 3, no. 1 (fall 1996): 1–19.

9. A good examination of the critical issues in this debate, especially as they bear on the use of television in dealing with serious issues, can be found in Jeffrey Alan Shandler, "While America Watches: Television and the Holocaust in the United States, from 1945 to the Present" (Ph.D. diss., Columbia University, 1995), 397–446.

10. Quoted in Doneson, *Holocaust in American Film,* 148–49.

11. This example is drawn from Edward T. Linenthal's excellent account of the making of the museum, *Preserving Memory: The Struggle to Create America's Holocaust Museum* (New York: Viking, 1995), 193–98.

12. The episode is described in Linenthal, *Preserving Memory,* 100–104.

13. James Young is the most perceptive interpreter of this iconographic landscape. See his *The Texture of Memory: Holocaust Memorials and Meaning* (New Haven, Conn.: Yale University Press, 1993).

2. TWO MODELS IN THE STUDY OF HOLOCAUST REPRESENTATION

1. See, for example, Arthur A. Cohen, *The Tremendum: A Theological Interpretation of the Holocaust* (New York: Crossroads, 1981); Emil Fackenheim, *Quest for Past and Present: Essays in Jewish Theology* (Bloomington: Indiana University Press, 1968); and *The Jewish Return into History: Reflections of the Age of Auschwitz and Jerusalem* (New York: Schocken Books, 1978).

2. I am using the term *constructivist* in a "soft" sense. I hold the fact of the murder of European Jewry and the manner in which it was carried out to be core facts about which there should be no basic disagreement. What is constructed is the meaning of those events and the way they are construed in individual and collective memory.

3. Alvin H. Rosenfeld, *A Double Dying: Reflections on Holocaust Literature* (Bloomington: Indiana University Press, 1980); Lawrence Langer, *The Holocaust and the Literary Imagination* (New Haven, Conn.: Yale University Press, 1975); Sidra DeKoven Ezrahi, *By Words Alone: The Holocaust in Literature* (Chicago: University of Chicago Press, 1980); David G. Roskies, *Against the Apocalypse: Responses to Catastrophe in Modern Jewish Culture* (Cambridge: Harvard University Press, 1984); Sara R. Horowitz, *Voicing the Void: Muteness and Memory in Holocaust Fiction* (Albany: State University

Notes

of New York Press, 1997); James E. Young, *Writing and Rewriting the Holocaust: Narrative and the Consequences of Interpretation* (Bloomington: Indiana University Press, 1988).

4. Lawrence L. Langer, ed., *Art from the Ashes* (New York: Oxford University Press, 1995) and David G. Roskies, ed., *The Literature of Destruction: Jewish Responses to Catastrophe* (Philadelphia: Jewish Publication Society, 1989).

5. These are, in order, Leyb Goldin, anonymous, Chaim Kaplan, and Rachel Auerbach, as they appear in Emmanuel Ringelblum, *Notes from the Warsaw Ghetto: The Journal of Emmanuel Ringelblum,* ed. and trans. Jacob Sloan (New York: Schocken Books, 1974), 422–564.

6. Langer, *Art from the Ashes,* 8.

7. Ibid., 6.

8. Ibid., 5.

9. Ibid., 554.

10. This is in fact the lens I attempted to provide in *ḤURBAN: Responses to Catastrophe in Hebrew Literature.*

11. Lawrence Langer, *Versions of Survival: The Holocaust and the Human Spirit* (Albany: State University of New York Press, 1982).

12. I am grateful to Sara Horowitz for this insight, presented in remarks delivered at the Association for Jewish Studies annual meeting in December 1998.

13. Tadeusz Borowski, *This Way for the Gas, Ladies and Gentlemen,* trans. Barbara Vedder (New York: Penguin Books, 1976), 121–22. Borowski wrote the stories contained in the volume in the year or two immediately after the war. He committed suicide in 1951. His work was first published in English translation in 1967.

14. Primo Levi, *Survival in Auschwitz,* trans. Stuart Woolf (New York: Collier Books, 1993). The book was written soon after the war; the original title was *Se questo è un uomo [If This Is a Man].* It appeared in English for the first time in 1960.

15. Primo Levi, *The Periodic Table,* trans. Raymond Rosenthal (New York: Schocken Books, 1984).

16. "A Conversation with Primo Levi by Philip Roth" in Levi, *Survival in Auschwitz,* 181.

17. Elie Wiesel, *Night,* trans. Stella Rodway (New York: Bantam Books, 1982), 62. *Night* first appeared in French in 1958 and in English in 1960.

18. Naomi Seidman, "Elie Wiesel and the Scandal of Jewish Rage," *Jewish Social Studies* (New Series), 3, no. 1 (fall 1996): 1–19.

Notes

19. Terrence Des Pres, *The Survivor: An Anatomy of Life in the Death Camps* (New York: Oxford University Press, 1976).

20. David Roskies, *The Jewish Search for a Usable Past* (Bloomington: Indiana University Press, 1999), chapter 3, "Ringelblum's Time Capsules."

21. Roskies, *Literature of Destruction*, 391.

22. Originally published in *Di goldene keyt* 46 (1963): 29–39. Translated by Leonard Wolf in Roskies, *Literature of Destruction*, 459–64.

23. Abraham Lewin, *A Cup of Tears*, ed. Anthony Polonsky, trans. Christopher Hutton (London: Blackwell, 1988).

24. Yehoshue Perle, "4580," trans. Elinor Robinson, in *The Literature of Destruction: Jewish Responses to Catastrophe,* ed. David G. Roskies (Philadelphia: Jewish Publication Society, 1989), 450–54.

25. Roskies, *Literature of Destruction*, 437.

26. Among the little we have in English is an imperfect edition of Ringelblum's own journal and one of his monographs: Ringelblum, *Warsaw Ghetto,* and Emanuel Ringelblum, *Polish-Jewish Relations During the Second World War,* ed. Joseph Kermish, Shmuel Krakowski, trans. Dafna Allon, Danuta Dabrowska, and Dana Keren (New York: Fertig, 1976).

27. Joseph Kermish, ed., *'Itonut hamahteret hayehudit bevarsha [The Jewish Underground Press in Warsaw],* trans. Ari Avner et al. (Jerusalem: Yad Vashem, 1979).

28. Lawrence Langer, *Admitting the Holocaust: Collected Essays* (New York: Oxford University Press: 1995). p. 57.

29. Ibid., 55.

30. For some constructive initial attempts in this direction, see Henry Greenspan, *On Listening to Holocaust Survivors: Recounting and Life History* (Westport, Conn.: Praeger, 1998), and David Patterson, *Along the Edge of Annihilation: The Collapse and Recovery of Life in the Holocaust Diary* (Seattle: University of Washington Press, 1999).

31. David Weiss Halivni, *The Book and the Sword: A Life of Learning in the Shadow of Destruction* (New York: Farrar, Straus & Giroux, 1996).

32. Ibid., 68.

3. THE HOLOCAUST AT THE MOVIES

1. The footage is probably more closely modeled on the film *Nazi Concentration Camps,* which was assembled for the first Nuremberg trial. See Jeffrey Shandler, *While America Watches: Televising the Holocaust* (New

Notes

York: Oxford University Press, 1999), chap. 1, for a fuller discussion of the screening of contemporary documentary footage.

2. Alain Renais's 1955 French-language film *Night and Fog* contains extensive documentary footage of the concentration camps, but it was never shown commercially in America. For perceptive remarks on war films and the Hollywood studios, see Ilan Avisar, *Screening the Holocaust* (Bloomington: Indiana University Press, 1988), 106–22.

3. It is only Jason Epstein, writing in *Commentary*, who finds these "mountains of bodies, recognizable faces, sexual organs, beaten children— mountains of them indiscriminately pushed, arms and legs swaying and wagging, by the bulldozer into a pit" to be "absolutely overpowering in their gigantic obscenity." Epstein is shocked because this is what mass death looks like in the twentieth century. "This is how it looked at Hiroshima . . . and this is how it may very well look tomorrow or a year from now" if the nuclear arms race is not constrained (*Commentary* 33 [January 1962]: 62). Epstein's review is published alongside a less favorable assessment by Harris Dienstfrey, an associate editor of *Commentary*. An editorial note justifies the "unusual step of presenting two differing responses" on the grounds that *Judgment at Nuremberg* "has provoked more heated discussion than any American movie within memory" and "makes a very ambitious attempt to deal with questions that are of particular interest to readers of *Commentary*."

4. The premier was covered as a news story in the *New York Times* on December 15, 1961, sec. C.

5. "Man's Long, Rough Pursuit of Justice," *Life*, December 15, 1965, 121–23.

6. Bosley Crowther, "Hollywood's Producer of Controversy," *New York Times Magazine*, December 10, 1961, 76–77.

7. Murray Schumach, "Hollywood Trial," *New York Times*, Sunday, April 30, 1961, II 9:1. For a good examination of how the daily coverage of the trial was handled on television, see Shandler, *While America Watches*, 83–132.

8. "Show Trial," *Time*, December 15, 1961, 85.

9. The television drama was generally well received. Claude Reines played the role of Judge Haywood and brought to the part a brooding intellectuality that was replaced in the movie by Spencer Tracy's stolid insistence on fair play. Also, the Marlene Dietrich character was absent from the teleplay, as of course was the possibility of a romantic connection with the judge. Serious critics generally felt that a high price was paid for expanding the project from 90 to 190 minutes.

Notes

10. Quoted by John C. Waugh, "Hollywood Letter," *Christian Science Monitor*, May 4, 1961.

11. Ibid.

12. Bosley Crowther, "Nuremberg Judgment," *New York Times*, December 24, 1961, p. x3.

13. Pauline Kael, *Kiss Kiss Bang Bang* (Boston: Little Brown, 1965, 1968), 206. Kael's chapter on Kramer ("The Intentions of Stanley Kramer") offers a jaundiced account of the producer-director's career; it is particularly good on *Ship of Fools*, which is another movie that deals with anti-Semitism and World War II.

14. Brendan Gill, "Current Cinema: Out of Evil," *New Yorker*, December 23, 1961, 68.

15. Gavin Lampert, "Judgment at Nuremberg," *Film Quarterly* 15, no. 2 (winter 1961–62): 51–52.

16. Philip T. Hartung, "The Screen: Who Shall Judge?" *Commonweal*, December 15, 1961: 318–19.

17. See Stanley Kauffmann, "Hollywood's Germany," *New Republic*, December 11, 1961, 26–27.

18. Arthur B. Clarke, "Judgment at Nuremberg," *Films in Review* 13, no. 1 (January 1962): 40.

19. Ibid.

20. Ronald Steel, "Kramer's Nuremberg," *Christian Century*, March 14, 1962, 32.

21. Clark, "Judgment," 41.

22. Tube, "Judgment at Nuremberg," *Variety*, October 18, 1961.

23. Gill, "Out of Evil," 68.

24. Jason Epstein, "Two Views of *Judgment at Nuremberg*," *Commentary* 33 (January 1962): 62.

25. Harris Dienstfrey, "Two Views of *Judgment at Nuremberg*," *Commentary* 33 (January 1962): 58.

26. Ibid.

27. Steel, "Kramer's Nuremberg."

28. "Man's Long, Rough Pursuit of Justice," *Life*, December 15, 1965, 123.

29. Kramer is quoted as saying that the film is "a reminder that what happened to some of those lower echelon defendants might happen to any citizens pressured by national expediency" (Waugh, "Hollywood Letter"). See Harris Dienstfrey's vigorous critique of the film's faulty parallels in *Commentary* 33 (January 1962): 58.

Notes

30. "Hollywood's Producer of Controversy," *New York Times Magazine,* December 10, 1961, 78.

31. Tube, "Judgment at Nuremberg."

32. Lawrence Langer, "The Americanization of the Holocaust on Stage and Screen," in *From Hester Street to Hollywood: The Jewish-American Stage and Screen,* ed. Sarah Blacher (Bloomington: Indiana University Press, 1985), 213–30; Judith Doneson, *The Holocaust in American Film* (Philadelphia: Jewish Publication Society, 1987); Avisar, *Screening the Holocaust.* I have learned much from Doneson's attention to the historical factors that shaped American films about the Holocaust and their audiences; my argument parallels hers in many respects.

33. Saul Freidlander, *Reflections on Nazism: An Essay on Kitsch and Death,* trans. Thomas Weyr (New York: Harper and Row, 1984).

34. Crowther, "Nuremberg Judgment."

35. Avisar, *Screening the Holocaust,* 122–25. Judith Doneson expresses some of the same criticisms, but her tone is less aggressive. See her *The Holocaust in American Film* (Philadelphia: Jewish Publication Society, 1987), 110–12.

36. David Desser and Lester D. Friedman, *American Jewish Filmmakers* (Urbana: University of Illinois Press, 1993), 167. See also Lester D. Friedman, *The Jewish Image in American Film,* (Secaucus, N.J.: Citadel Press, 1987); Frank R. Cunningham, *Sidney Lumet: Film and Literary Vision* (Lexington: University Press of Kentucky, 1991); and Jay Boyer, *Sidney Lumet* (New York: Twayne, 1993).

37. Louis Chapin, "Pawnbroker," *Christian Science Monitor,* May 22, 1965.

38. Brendan Gill, *New Yorker,* April 24, 1965, 164–65.

39. Bosley Crowther, "Screen: *The Pawnbroker* Opens at Three Theaters," *New York Times,* Wednesday, April 14, 1965.

40. Ibid.

41. Gill, *New Yorker,* April 24, 1965, 165.

42. Brendan Gill represented the apogee of this admiration when he wrote in the *New Yorker* (April 24, 1965), "By far the most distinguished thing about *The Pawnbroker* is Rod Steiger's performance in the title role. It comes close to being true indeed, that he *is The Pawnbroker* as well as the pawnbroker, with the result that much of what I didn't like about the picture has already begun to slip from my mind, dimmed and blurred against the general brightness and force of its star." The admiration, however, was not universal. Stanley Kauffmann finds Steiger "bound in the involutions of the Actor's Studio; we are aware of internal devices being used for a

Notes

kind of self-flagellation which may, if all goes well, also affect us—instead of a direct actor-audience relation." *New Republic,* April 24, 1965.

43. Again, celebrated but not by all. In a harshly critical review of the film Robert Hatch finds that "there doesn't seem to be a word of truth in it." Of the opening sequence in which Nazerman recalls a family picnic interrupted by a Nazi dragnet, Hatch writes, "And I was carried off into the bucolic world of cigarette advertising by the flash-back idyll (project in slow motion to emphasize its unearthly loveliness) that sets the stage for the coming misery. . . . The Jews of Germany were not much given to conspicuous country revels at the time when Hitler's exterminator packs were roaming the country, and the trite sentimentality of the scene seems a heartless parody of what they suffered. It is not conceived out of conviction or artistic necessity: it is a pitch to the customer. And that, I'm afraid, sums up the picture." Robert Hatch, "Films: *The Pawnbroker," The Nation,* May 10, 1965, 515–16.

44. Philip T. Hartung, "The Screen: Harlem, Mon Amour," *Commonweal* 82 (May 14, 1965), 255–56.

45. Annette Insdorf stresses the sophisticated editing of the movie and credits Lumet and editor Ralph Rosenbaum with the "use of montage as a complex visual analogue for mental processes." *Indelible Shadows* (New York: Random House, 1983), 23.

46. Albert Bermel, "Frenzy in a Void," *Midstream* 11, no. 2 (June 1965), 65.

47. Stanley Kauffmann, "Melpomene in Harlem," *New Republic* 152 (April 24, 1965): 24.

48. The speech in the film is substantially the same as that in the novel. Edward Lewis Wallant, *The Pawnbroker* (New York: Manor Books, 1962), 43.

49. Bermel, 63.

50. Ibid., 66.

51. Avisar, *Screening the Holocaust,* 124.

52. Wallant, *Pawnbroker,* 206. (These are the novel's concluding words.)

53. Crowther, *"The Pawnbroker."*

54. Chapin, "Pawnbroker."

55. Insdorf, *Indelible Shadows,* 24.

56. Sidney Lumet, "Keep Them on the Hook," *Film Quarterly* 2 (1966): 17.

57. Avisar, *Screening the Holocaust,* 124.

58. A valuable comparison of the reception of the two works can be

Notes

found in Jeffrey Shandler, "Schindler's Discourse: America Discusses the Holocaust and Its Mediation, from NBC'S Miniseries to Spielberg's Film" in Yosefa Loshistsky, *Spielberg's Holocaust* (Bloomington: Indiana University Press, 1997), 153–71. For a fuller account of the responses to *Holocaust* in the context of representation of the Holocaust on television, see Shandler's *While America Watches*.

59. The consensus is by no means absolute. The conclusion of the miniseries was much less a happy ending than that of the film. In the *Village Voice* symposium on *Schindler's List* J. Hoberman remarks, "There's one sense that *Holocaust, the Miniseries* was more naturalistic than *Schindler's List*. As I recall, the central Jewish family has maybe six children and five of them die. These are characters who, if one watches, one is invested in. But in *Schindler's List* virtually every character in whom the audience has emotional investment lives!" *Village Voice*, March 29, 1994, 31.

60. John Gross, "Hollywood and the Holocaust," *New York Review of Books* 16, no. 3 (February 3, 1994): 3–5.

61. Stanley Kauffmann, *New Republic* 210, no. 4 (January 24, 1994): 27.

62. Julie Salamon, "Spielberg's Portrait of a Holocaust Hero," *Wall Street Journal*, December 16, 1993, sec. A, p. 14.

63. David Danby, "Unlikely Hero," *New York Magazine,* December 15, 1993.

64. Janet Maslin, "Imagining the Holocaust to Remember It," *New York Times*, December 15, 1993, sec. C, p. 19; Terrence Rafferty, "A Man of Transactions," *New Yorker*, December 20, 1993, 129–32.

65. Gross, "Hollywood and the Holocaust."

66. Stanley Kauffmann, "Spielberg Revisited," *New Republic*, January 24, 1994, 26–27.

67. Rafferty, "Man of Transactions."

68. Maslin, "Imagining the Holocaust."

69. Denby, "Unlikely Hero."

70. Gross, "Hollywood and the Holocaust."

71. Maslin, "Imagining the Holocaust."

72. Steven G. Kellman, "*Schindler's List:* Spielberg's Homecoming," *Midstream* 40, no. 2 (Febuary/March 1994): 12.

73. Mordecai Newman, "Spielberg's Bar Mitzvah," *Jewish Frontier* 61, no. 1 (January/February 1994): 23.

74. Maslin, "Imagining the Holocaust."

75. Rafferty, "Man of Transactions."

76. Kauffmann, "Spielberg Revisited," 27.

Notes

77. Rafferty, "Man of Transactions," 132.

78. Gross, "Hollywood and the Holocaust."

79. Robert Galately, "Between Exploitation, Rescue, and Annihilation: Reviewing *Schindler's List,*" *Central European History* 26, no. 4 (1993): 475–89.

80. Ibid., 487.

81. The Maslin review ("Imagining the Holocaust") appeared on December 15, 1993, and the Rich piece more than two weeks later. Frank Rich, "Extras in the Shadows," *New York Times,* January 2, 1994.

82. Gross's review appeared in the February 4, 1994, issue, and Epstein's eleven weeks later. Jason Epstein, "A Dissent on *Schindler's List,*" *New York Review of Books,* April 21, 1994, 65.

83. Kauffmann's first review appeared in the December 13, 1993, issue, and Wieseltier's column as the end piece for the January 24, 1994, issue, which also contains a second, positive review by Kauffmann ("Spielberg Revisited"). Stanley Kauffmann, *New Republic,* December 13, 1993, 26–27. Leon Wieseltier, "Close Encounters of the Nazi Kind," *New Republic,* January 24, 1994, 42.

84. Michael André Bernstein, "The *Schindler's List* Effect," *American Scholar* 63, no. 3 (summer 1994): 429.

85. Philip Gourevitch, "A Dissent on *Schindler's List,*" *Commentary* 97, no. 2 (February 1994): 49.

86. Wieseltier, "Close Encounters."

87. I take the term "critical intellectuals" from Miriam Bratu Hansen's valuable study of the reception of *Schindler's List* ("*Schindler's List* Is Not *Shoah:* Second Commandment, Popular Modernism, and Public Memory" in *Spielberg's Holocaust: Critical Perspectives on Schindler's List,* ed. Yosefa Loshitzky (Bloomington: Indiana University Press: 1997), 77–103.

88. The letter of Norbert Friedman of West Hempstead, New York, in the "Letters from Readers" section, *Commentary* 97, no. 6 (June 1994): 3. There are many similar responses that go on to label Gourevitch's criticisms as nitpicking in the face of Spielberg's great achievement.

89. Insdorf's remarks are contained in a symposium moderated by J. Hoberman ("Spielberg, the Holocaust and Memory") in the *Village Voice,* March 29, 1994, 29. The participants were Wanda Bershen, Richard Goldstein, J. Hoberman, Annette Insdorf, Ken Jacobs, Gertrud Koch, Art Spiegelman, and James Young.

90. Ibid.

91. Among elite audiences, there is a preferred competitor to *Schindler's*

Notes

List: Claude Lanzmann's *Shoah*. As we shall see shortly, *Shoah*, for all its differences, is also a film that implies that its treatment of its subject is definitive.

92. Gourevitch, "Dissent on *Schindler's List*," 51.

93. See Bernstein, "*Schindler's List* Effect," 429: "Perhaps the most succinct way to register the kinds of qualms with which I left the theater is simply to ask why *Schindler's List* is so complicit with the Hollywood convention of showing catastrophe primarily from the point of view of the perpetrators."

94. Sara Horowitz, "But Is It Good for the Jews? Spielberg's Schindler and the Aesthetics of Atrocity," in *Spielberg's Holocaust: Critical Perspectives on Schindler's List,* ed. Yosefa Loshitzky (Bloomington: Indiana University Press: 1997), 125–26. Gourevitch recounts that Spielberg's casting team placed ads in the Warsaw papers seeking "about 800 people, especially families, who look stereotypically Semitic ("Dissent on *Schindler's List*," 51) and stresses the congruence between these body images and the caricatures in *Der Stuermer,* the infamous anti-Semitic magazine in inter-war Germany. Great offense was taken to this remark in subsequent letters to the editor.

95. See Horowitz's nuanced explication of this scene in "Is It Good for the Jews?" 125–26. Among the many things left out, Horowitz also makes a point of stressing the grinding hunger of daily life in the ghetto, which, though less sensational, had a greater demoralizing impact than the random shootings represented in the film. See also Molly Magid Hoagland, "What *Schindler* Missed," *Midstream* 40, no. 3 (April 1994): 32–35, and Gourevitch, "Dissent on *Schindler's List*," 51.

96. Jason Epstein, "A Dissent on *Schindler's List*," *New York Review of Books* 12, no. 8 (April 21, 1994): 65.

97. Ibid.

98. See Omer Bartov, "Spielberg's Oskar: Hollywood Tries Evil" in *Spielberg's Holocaust: Critical Perspectives on Schindler's List,* ed. Yosefa Loshitzky (Bloomington: Indiana University Press: 1997), 46: "Thus, a relatively minor, and quite extraordinary case has been transformed into a representative segment of the 'story' as a whole, obliterating, or at least neglecting the fact that in the 'real' Holocaust, most of the Jews died, most of the Germans collaborated with the perpetrators or remained passive bystanders, most of the victims sent to the showers were gassed, and most of the survivors did not walk across green meadows to Palestine."

99. Bernstein, "*Schindler's List* Effect," 430.

Notes

100. Wieseltier, "Close Encounters," 42.

101. Horowitz, "Is It Good for the Jews?" 123.

102. Ibid., 122.

103. Gourevitch, "Dissent on *Schindler's List*," 50.

104. Ibid., 51.

105. Hoagland, "What *Schindler* Missed," 35.

106. Horowitz, "Is It Good for the Jews?" 128.

107. Ibid., 130. On this same subject see the illuminating remarks in Judith E. Doneson, "The Image Lingers: The Feminization of the Jew in *Schindler's List*" in *Spielberg's Holocaust: Critical Perspectives on Schindler's List,* ed. Yosefa Loshitzky (Bloomington: Indiana University Press: 1997), 140–52.

108. These issues are examined in Saul Friedlander, ed., *Probing the Limits of Representation: Nazism and the "Final Solution"* (Cambridge: Harvard University Press, 1992).

109. Wieseltier, "Close Encounters," 42.

110. Symposium on *Schindler's List, Village Voice,* March 29, 1994, 30.

111. Claude Lanzmann's comments first appeared in *Le Monde,* March 3, 1994; they were reprinted in translation in "Why Spielberg Has Distorted the Truth," *Guardian Weekly* (U.K.), April 3, 1994, 14.

112. Symposium on *Schindler's List, Village Voice,* March 29, 1994, 27.

113. Bartov, "Spielberg's Oskar," 55.

114. Hansen, "*Schindler's List* Is Not *Shoah*," 94.

115. Elazar Barkan, review of *Schindler's List, American Historical Review* 99, no. 4 (October 1994): 1248.

116. Alvin Rosenfeld, *The Americanization of the Holocaust* (Ann Arbor: University of Michigan Press, 1995), 25–38.

117. Lawrence L. Langer, *Versions of Survival* (Albany: State University of New York Press, 1982), 1–65.

118. See Bryan Cheyette, "The Holocaust in the Picture-House," *Times Literary Supplement* no. 4742 (February 18, 1994): 18.

119. See Gourevitch, "Dissent on *Schindler's List*," 51.

120. Given the prevalence of Christian material in the film, it is interesting how little note was taken of it by the mass of Jewish viewers and their communal organizations.

121. Stephen Schiff, "Behind the Camera: Seriously Spielberg," *New Yorker,* March 21, 1994, 97.

122. Quoted in Schiff, "Seriously Spielberg."

Notes

4. THE FUTURE OF MEMORIALIZATION

1. James Young, *The Texture of Memory: Holocaust Memorials and Meaning* (New Haven: Yale University Press, 1993), 1–15.

2. Peter Novick, *The Holocaust in American Life* (Boston: Houghton Mifflin, 1999).

3. Ibid., 195.

4. Ibid., 176–77.

5. A similar point is made by Tony Judt in an insightful review of Novick's *Holocaust in American Life*. "The Morbid Truth," *New Republic*, July 19 and 26, 1999, 40.

6. See Stanley Fish, *Is There a Text in This Class? The Authority of Interpretive Communities* (Cambridge: Harvard University Press, 1980).

7. I take the example from Rona Sheramy, "Defining Lessons: Holocaust Education and American Jewish Youth from World War II to the Present" (Ph.D. diss., Brandeis University, 2000).

Index

Index

Index

docudramas, 23–26, 132–34
Doneson, Judith E., 188n6

education about Holocaust, 33–34, 76–79, 162, 173–78
Eichmann in Jerusalem (Arendt's book), 14
Eichmann trial, 11–14, 92–93
Epstein, Jason, 98, 134, 140–41, 192n3
exceptionalist model: camp literature, 62–63; ghetto literature, 70–71; Langer's anthology, 44, 49–53, 54–56; museum missions, 76, 78; overview, 38–41; survivor narratives and, 75; synthesizing with constructivist model, 79–83; university studies, 77, 78–79
Exodus (Uris's book), 14

Facing History and Ourselves (curriculum), 34
Fiennes, Ralph (as A. Goeth), 129, 143–44
Film Quarterly, 95
Fortunoff Video Archive, 181, 183
Frank, Anne, 16–19
Frank, Otto, 18
Freed, James Ingo, 31
Freidlander, Saul, 105

Galately, Robert, 132–34
Garland, Judy (as I. Hoffman), 94–95, 96, 99
Gardner, Ava, 94
ghetto analogy in *Pawnbroker*, 124–25

ghetto literature: constructivist approach to, 63–71; invisibility in *Schindler's List*, 138–39; proposed scholarly approach, 80; Ringelblum archive, 47–48, 64, 66, 67, 68–69. *See also* canon of Holocaust literature
The Ghost Writer (Roth's book), 82
Gill, Brendan, 95, 97–98, 112, 194–95n42
Goeth, Amon, 129, 136, 143–44
Goodrich, Frances, 18–19
Gourevitch, Philip, 135, 136, 138–39, 142–43, 198n94
Green, Gerald, 25
Gross, John, 127, 128, 129, 131, 132

Hackett, Albert, 18–19
Halivni, David Weiss, 72–75
Hall of Remembrance, 31
Hansen, Miriam Bratu, 146–47
Hartman, Geoffrey, 141
Hartung, Philip T., 115
Hatch, Robert, 195n43
Haywood, Dan (film character), 86–91, 94, 95, 105, 107
Hellman, Lillian, 18
Hirsch, Helen, 143–44
Hoagland, Molly Magid, 143
Hoberman, J., 196n59
Hochhuth, Rolf, 12
Hoffman, Irene, 99
Holocaust Council, 27–29
Holocaust Education Center, 33
The Holocaust in American Film (Doneson's book), 188n6
The Holocaust in American Life (Novick's book), 164–65, 187n1

Index

Holocaust Memorial Museum, U.S., 4, 23, 26–33, 130–31
Holocaust Testimonies: The Ruins of Memory (Langer's book), 182–83
Holocaust (TV mini-series), 23–26, 35, 93, 125–26, 196*n*59
hope themes: A. Frank's diary, 19; camp literature, 58–60; Holocaust Museum, 31–32
Horowitz, Sara, 139, 143, 144, 198*n*95

identity of Jewish people: Holocaust preoccupation and, 162–63; *Judgment at Nuremberg,* 103–4
Indelible Shadows (Insdorf's book), 124
individual heroism theme in *Schindler's List,* 140–41, 149–51
Inherit the Wind (Kramer's film), 93
Insdorf, Annette, 124, 136–37, 195*n*45
interpretive community model of memorialization, 171–78
Irving Thalberg Award, 92
Israel: Eichmann trial, 11; Entebbe rescue, 25; role in avoidance of Holocaust, 7–8; Six-Day War, 14–16; use of Holocaust, 164

Janning, Ernst (film character), 87, 95
Jewish Frontier, 131
Jewish identity in representations: A. Frank's diary, 18; Holocaust Museum, 27–29; *Judgment at*

Nuremberg, 103–4; television mini-series, 24. *See also The Pawnbroker* (Lumet's film)
Judaism in America: Christian community change toward, 12–13; criticisms of Holocaust preoccupation, 161–65; Holocaust avoidance and, 9, 75
Judgment at Nuremberg (Kramer's film): American messages, 90–91, 101–2, 104, 108–9, 150–51; casting purposes, 94–97; concentration camp footage, 85–86; filmmaker's approach, 86–91; invisibility of Jewish people, 103–4; Kramer's comments on, 102, 193*n*29; photos, 88, 106; release/reception, 91–94, 192*n*3, 192*n*9; unintended messages, 105–7; universal messages, 86, 89–90, 97–101

Kael, Pauline, 95, 193*n*13
Kaplan, Chaim, 68
Katzenberg, Jeffrey, 156–57
Kauffmann, Stanley: *Judgment at Nuremberg,* 95; *Pawnbroker,* 116–17, 194–95*n*42; *Schindler's List,* 127, 129, 132
Kaufman, Boris, 125
Kellman, Steven G., 131
Keneally, Thomas, 138, 142–43
Kermish, Joseph, 69
Kingsley, Ben, 128
Kiss Kiss Bang Bang (Kael's book), 193*n*13
Koch, Gertrud, 145
Korczak, Janusz, 66, 71

Index

Index

Index

Index